Psychological and Psychiatric Problems in Men

There is a plethora of books about the psychological, social and sexual problems besetting women; and a handful claim to examine male–female differences, but they are all written from a feminist perspective and focus on women. By contrast, this book provides an unbiased, objective account of a grossly neglected subject area: the psychological, social and sexual problems besetting men. It is based on an analysis of societal influences as well as developmental, anatomical and physio-logical factors, and it incorporates the latest research in medicine and gender studies.

The issues discussed are highly topical. The author is concerned with aggression, violence and criminality, with sexuality, both 'deviant' and 'normal', and with problems such as alcohol and drug dependence. Explanations are put forward for all these phenomena and remedies suggested for those that require them. The differential incidence and presentation of major and minor psychiatric illness in males is described, and the respective roles of drug regimes and psychotherapies are fully investigated.

Psychological and Psychiatric Problems in Men will be essential reading for all health professionals, for social workers and for welfare officers in the universities, in the armed forces and in the prison system. It will also form an important resource for medical students taking their psychiatry block.

Joan Gomez is a highly respected consultant psychiatrist in a busy London practice. She has long experience of prison work and is currently involved in counselling people with AIDS. She has published widely in journals and has several books to her name, including *Liaison Psychiatry*, Croom Helm, 1987.

Psychological and Psychiatric Problems in Men

Joan Gomez

London and New York

First published in 1991
by Routledge
11 New Fetter Lane, London EC4P 4EE

Simultaneously published in the USA and Canada
by Routledge
29 West 35th Street, New York, NY 10001

First published in paperback in 1993

© 1991 Joan Gomez

Typeset by LaserScript Limited, Mitcham, Surrey
Printed and bound in Great Britain by
Mackays of Chatham PLC, Chatham, Kent

British Library Cataloguing in Publication Data
Gomez, Joan
    Psychological and psychiatric problems in men.
    1. Men. Psychology
    I. Title
    155.632

Library of Congress Cataloging in Publication Data
Gomez, Joan.
    Psychological and psychiatric problems in men/Joan Gomez.
    p. cm.
    Includes bibliographical references and index.
    1. Men–Mental health. 2 Men–Psychology. I. Title.
    RC451.4.M45G66 1990
    155.6'32–dc20   90-8718
                                                            CIP

ISBN 0–415–02336–X
    0–415–09713–4 (pbk)

Contents

Chapter one

La difference

Men are different. Yet they are people, too. Women's physical and emotional characteristics and sufferings have been studied, written about and mulled over – and over. By contrast, the problems particularly affecting men are neglected – even by themselves. Men make far less use than women of the whole range of health care services except those concerned with accidents, alcohol and sexually-transmitted diseases. They consult doctors, psychiatrists and social workers less often, spend fewer days in bed and far fewer off work than females in similar circumstances. In planning a psychiatric facility, for example, twice as many places must be allowed for women as for men. Yet in the final analysis men are the sicker sex. They die sooner and suffer more of the serious chronic diseases as well as the sudden, death-dealing disasters such as coronary thrombosis. Psychological disorders affecting men are frequently more dramatic, often dangerous and likely to have far-reaching results.

Psychopathy, drug dependency, delusional aggression and sexual deviations are all much commoner in males. While women take overdoses and live to tell the tale, men are likely to commit suicide using violent means. Adolescent delinquency, and crime, whatever its causes, are mainly male problems: not through lesser moral rectitude but because of a greater propensity for energetic action. Schizophrenia, the major psychiatric scourge, affects the sexes equally but strikes earlier in the male and is more severe. While most families can cope with a schizophrenic daughter at home, even the most devoted parents – or wife – find a son with the same disorder too difficult to live with. At the end of the road, more than 90 per cent of the homeless and hopeless down-and-outs who wander the urban wilderness are men. Schizophrenia, alcoholism and personality problems beset this group.

In western culture men suffer less than women from the standard neuroses and minor psychiatric disorders (Briscoe 1982) but workaholism is predominantly male, and so is its sequel, burnout. Mood disorders affect women more than men in the west, but the most disturbing of them – mania – more often affects men, and with a greater risk of appalling consequences. An energetic man with delusions of enormous power and wealth may be in a position to destroy his company or his government. Among the psychosomatic disorders women have a corner in headache, nervous stomach, eating disorders and high blood pressure, while men under stress may develop peptic ulcers, asthma or ischaemic heart disease. This is the situation in the west. In developing countries such as India, Uganda and New Guinea, men suffer more than women from all types of mental problems including depressive illness – in sharp contrast. In South America the situation is again opposite with psychologically-disturbed women easily outnumbering the men. This may be due to the machismo concept, making it unacceptable for a man to show physical weakness or admit to anxieties or depressive thoughts.

The big question is to what extent the differing tendencies between males and females are biologically based, and how much is due to social expectations and early learning experiences. Sex roles are taught by parents and society, but biological sex itself makes boys and girls respond differently. As important as what adults attempt to teach is what the children themselves choose to learn. Anti-establishment and feminist activists make angry and agonized attempts to recast the male and female moulds. Yet the stereotypes remain, dented but not badly damaged, even in decadent western circles. The ineradicable male qualities of height and muscularity and the more efficient use of fuel by the muscles, regardless of any training programmes, are admired and sought after still. Even in today's sophisticated society, material success is positively statistically associated with above-average height. This has led ambitious parents to attempt to buy growth hormone injections to make their sons grow taller. Male athleticism means fame, honour, hero-worship and for the few, a great deal of money. Women cannot compete in this sphere, particularly obvious in tennis. With this biological headstart, unhampered by cyclical hormone swings, pregnancy and what follows, it is not surprising that men retain the dominant role.

In agricultural communities men and women have separate tasks, appropriate to their physical strength. But in modern urban society, even where affluence and technology have diminished the value of muscle power, men still play most of the leading roles. Even as children boys prefer to play with their own sex, while little girls enjoy playing with either. The same situation is replayed later with men's clubs or sports activities, but with no equally pleasurable retreat for women together. Men also have an awareness of their scarcity value. Their lives are spangled with dangers from Day One. Despite the risks of childbirth, women have consistently outnumbered men since the late Middle Ages. Only in 1987 in the UK did the balance shift: in one age range, 15–29, there are more males (Dixon 1987).

Sandra Bem (1981), writing from a feminist viewpoint, has studied the psychological attributes which differentiate between the sexes:

Males score high on:

   assertiveness
   analytical ability
   independence
   athleticism
   self-reliance
   combativeness
   toughness
   leadership
   physical courage
   moral courage
   ability to solve problems
   emotional reticence

Females excel in:

   emotional expressivity
   intuition
   adaptability
   nurturance
   patience
   reliability
   tact
   helpfulness
   sympathy
   reasonableness

Obviously all these qualities are present to some extent in everyone, but the trend is clear. The most crude male and female stereotypes are constantly presented by the media, particularly in advertising. Women are seen as interested almost exclusively in hairsprays, laundry, floor-cleaning and slimming – and the story-line is romance. Men are targeted for alcoholic drinks, cars, business and travel, with male chauvinism portrayed in those who use the product. Television plays are dominated by action men: fierce, fearless and – for all we can tell – illiterate. Women are slim, and dim.

The Type *A* go-getting, dynamic personality is something only men aspire to, in spite of its reputation for bringing on sudden death. This is an example of the risk-taking behaviour men cannot resist and little boys practise in advance. The reasons for the better health and survival rates of married compared with single men rest in the sensible caring and restraining influence of the other sex.

Chapter two

Biological aspects

Men in the main are bigger and stronger than women, and usually more competitive, aggressive and actively interested in sex, as remarked by Darwin more than a century ago. These traits are among many that are biologically-based. Male/female differences are present from the moment of conception and develop dramatically during life before birth and again, with renewed vigour, at puberty. The changes are guided by the powerful sex steroids, organizing and differentiating the tissues prenatally, activating them from adolescence onwards. Anatomical development of the genital organs is only one area influenced by the sex hormones before birth. There are also far-reaching effects on attitudes and behaviour in childhood and beyond. For example, if a girl baby has been exposed to male hormones as a foetus, or suffers from congenital adrenal hyperplasia which has the same result, she is likely to grow into an energetic, tomboyish girl, more interested in cars than dolls, in career than marriage (Baker 1980). It follows that sex-hormone factors operating before birth as well as later determine the way in which psychological problems and disorders differ between the sexes. Paranoid delusions in a schizophrenic man, for example, are far likelier to lead to physical violence than in a women patient. There are no female equivalents of Peter Sutcliffe, the schizophrenic murderer of many women.

Early development and later effects

Male programming begins with the Y-chromosome from the sperm, the essential determiner of sex. The basic structure of every foetus is female, until the Y-chromosome, if present, produces special modifications. If there is a Y-chromosome, the embryo is male no matter how many X-chromosomes he may have, as, for instance in Klinefelter's syndrome (XXY). The masculinizing effect of the Y-chromosome is mediated through HY-antigen, attached to the short arm of the Y-chromosome near the centromere. The amount of HY-antigen depends on the number of Y-chromosomes, and is increased in males of 47 (XYY) karyotype, compared with the usual 46 (XY) arrangement. In human twin pairs of different sexes, the female may be slightly more masculine than most, because of seepage through the placenta of the magical HY antigen. In the equivalent 'freemartin' cattle or sheep the female twin is sterile, but this does not apply to humans. The male twin is, of course, unaffected. It has been found that among a significant proportion of male transsexuals, there are abnormally low levels of HY antigen (Engel *et al.* 1980; Spoljar *et al.* 1981).

HY antigen sets off the whole developmental sequence with the germinal ridge of the embryo forming the testes. These embryonic testes are already producing testosterone, the most important male sex hormone, from the seventh week after conception. Its essential action at this stage, helped by another male hormone, Mullerian inhibiting factor, is to suppress the development of the female type of reproductive apparatus, and to impose the male pattern. Testosterone is secreted by the Leydig cells of the testis. These are plentiful in the foetus and newborn, their production stimulated by hormones from the placenta. The descent of the testes from the abdomen requires supplies of testosterone from the Leydig cells. Soon after birth these cells almost disappear, to increase in number again at puberty. They comprise about 20 per cent of the adult testis. Testosterone output hits its maximum at about age 20, and falls off very gradually, reaching 50 per cent of its top value at 60 plus. There is a wide individual variation, however, completely unrelated to the masculine stereotype of athletic appearance. Mullerian inhibiting factor, made in the Sertoli cells of the testis, guides the formation of the testicular extras: the epididymus, seminal vesicle, and vas deferens or sperm tube, on each side.

The development of the brain and nervous system

Before and shortly after birth there is active growth and development in the brain and nervous system, divergent in the two sexes. Testosterone and its potent conversion product, dihydrotestosterone, act in the male to modify the basic female blueprint. The speech cortex in the left temporal lobe of the brain has developed by the twentieth week in the womb, and is smaller in the male. On the other hand his visuospatial cortex in the right hemisphere, concerned with assessing three-dimensional relationships, develops earlier than in the female and is more highly elaborated. Even in the pre-school stage the differing abilities of boys and girls are noticeable. Little boys of 3 or 4 show more skill and enjoyment in building with Lego and the like than little girls, but with two-dimensional jigsaws the sexes cope equally. Boys usually have better binocular vision throughout life, also relevant to constructional aptitude. The male brain, on average, is larger than the female, by about 150ml in the adult, but the cerebral circulation is faster in females and they have proportionately more grey matter. They also have more connections between the two sides of the brain, served by a larger splenium in the corpus callosum, the main bridge between the hemispheres. Because of their different and asymmetrical brain development, males tend to excel in mathematical reasoning and such skills as map-reading, while females do better in the use of words, rote learning and perceptual speed and dexterity. Differences between the sexes in interests, outlook and activities are also influenced by the sex hormones, but there is a huge learning factor which clouds the biological effects (Flor-Henry 1983). Faced with an intellectual problem or other stress, men pour out more of the activating neurotransmitters, dopamine and noradrenaline, than women. However, the actual performance in meeting the challenge is about equal. This variation in brain–chemical response between the sexes may be a matter of biology, or perhaps men are programmed by their upbringing to react energetically to problems calling for mental effort. Women might be expected, by tradition, to be alerted particularly by the cry of a child or a person in pain. It is well known that, for whatever reason, mothers – and grandmothers – wake at the sound of their baby's cry, while fathers sleep on.

Puberty and after

No one knows precisely what sets off puberty, but it is probably a pattern of signals from various parts of the brain, impinging on the hypothalamus. At this stage it starts producing luteinizing hormone releasing factor, LHRH, for the first time. This in turn stimulates the pituitary to make luteinizing hormone, LH, and follicle-stimulating hormone, FSH, the two hormones which control the reproductive apparatus in the adult. Their effect is cyclical in the female but sustained in the male. In the testes, LH brings on the increase in testosterone-producing Leydig cells, and FSH controls sperm production. While the pituitary continues making LH and FSH from puberty lifelong, testosterone levels decline gradually from middle adulthood. From their late 50s most men notice, and often worry about, a fall-off in sexual performance. The average age for giving up intercourse is 68. Both the dramatic developments at puberty and the gentle climacteric decline depend largely on the amount of available testosterone. There is no male equivalent to the sharp cut off of fertility at the female menopause.

Between the ages of 13 and 20 testosterone stimulates the penis, scrotum and testes to enlarge eightfold. It induces the larynx to get larger and the skin all over the body to grow thicker, with increased activity of the sebaceous glands causing acne in some. The bones are considerably strengthened by the deposition of calcium salts, and there is a specific effect on the shape of the pelvis. It lengthens to a funnel with a narrowed outlet – well adapted for load-bearing. Most important in male adolescents is an increase in muscle mass to almost double, with more proteinous tissue all over the body. The musculature in the upper part of the body is much more powerful than that of the female, even if the latter is athletically trained. Because of its marked effect in building muscle, testosterone or its analogues, the anabolic steroids, are widely used by athletes to improve their performance. They are also used in a somewhat dubious way in the hope of increasing strength and vigour in elderly men. While testosterone causes a spurt in total body growth during puberty, it also encourages the closing off of the epiphyses of the long bones. The result is that the final height of a man is slightly less than it would have been had he been deprived of testosterone. Castration, an age-old method of preventing the production of male hormone, is used to make domestic animals more docile, and was used also to make men more amenable to slavery from the Middle Bronze Age. It was continued to provide male sopranos for the Sistine Choir until the death of Pope Pius IX in 1879.

Eunuchs tend to be taller and more willowy than normal men, with wider hips and fatter abdomens and thighs. Their skin is more delicate and head hair more luxuriant, while body hair is scant and there is no beard. The vocal cords are nearer the female or child's size. Normally, at age 6 the cords are approximately 10mm long in both sexes, but they grow faster in boys from about 12. By 20 the male cords are 24mm long compared with 16mm for the female, and at 30 the difference is maintained at 30 and 20mm respectively. The slow development of the laryngeal apparatus accounts for the relatively late age at which bass singers reach their peak.

As the testes become more active, the basic metabolic rate increases by 5-10 per cent making adolescent boys less prone to puppy fat than girls. Male hormone also accounts for the greater number and density of red blood cells in men, increasing the oxygen-carrying capacity of the blood. Less desirable is the propensity to baldness. Providing a man has the genetic background for baldness, he will lose his hair only if he secretes substantial quantities of androgens. Women may develop male-type baldness if they have an androgenic tumour. Pubic and axillary hair grows in slightly different patterns in the two sexes, under the influence of androgens from the adrenal glands.

Psychological aspects of developmental anomalies

Variations and deviations in male sexuality and attitudes are reviewed in Chapters 12 and 13. At least part of the symptomatology relates to prenatal influences. If a diabetic mother is given female sex hormones to maintain her pregnancy, her child, if male, is likely to grow up less boisterous than most, and his choice of toys less warlike. Male transsexuals are thought to lack HY antigen from before birth, and degrees of homosexuality are thought to correlate with unusually low or high levels of testosterone or oestrogen impinging on the foetus, or to lack of responsiveness to androgens (Dorner 1979). The way in which social, cultural and individual family influences interact with biological tendencies is complex and not well understood. Major chromosome disorders as in Klinefelter's and the Fragile-X syndromes are also relevant (Chapter 4).

Susceptibility to disease

The ways in which men differ from women in their vulnerability to psychiatric disorders is dealt with in detail throughout the book, but two common variants or exaggerations of biological make-up which occur more often in boys deserve a mention here – dyslexia and hyperactivity. They are inconvenient and cause anxiety, especially to parents, but in neither condition is there evidence of brain damage or disease, or even of difficulty in concentrating if the child's interest is engaged. Boys, more often than girls, may lie at the lower end of the continuum of those with high or low verbal skills. Similarly, while most children are restless when they are bored, boys are generally livelier than girls, and there is usually nothing mentally abnormal about a hyperactive boy.

The risks of physical disease differ between the sexes, beginning before birth, with males the more susceptible. More male foetuses than female are spontaneously aborted, and the stillbirth and neonatal mortality in the west runs at 120 males to 100 females. Because of the linkage to the X-chromosome of some of the genes associated with immunity, males, having only one X-chromosome may be at a disadvantage in dealing, for instance with infection. Women in general have higher immunoglobulin levels than men, and they do not suffer from immunoglobulin deficiency disorders. Men gain in being less susceptible to such auto-immune diseases as rheumatoid arthritis and Hashimoto's thyroiditis. They are also less likely to develop other thyroid problems or anaemia. Men are not only more at risk from infection, but more importantly from all the cancers except those affecting the breasts and female reproductive system. Lymphoma and leukaemia are especially common in males because of their less efficient immunity arrangements. It may be that the much greater prevalence of HIV infection and AIDS in men in the west, albeit mainly homosexuals, is enhanced for the same biological reason.

Of the sixty-four commonest causes of death in the USA, in fifty-seven the mortality rate is higher for men. With the advent of antibiotics the high death rate from infection that formerly reduced drastically the number of young men no longer applies, but in industrial societies males of 15-24 suffer an excess of violent and accidental deaths. These include road traffic accidents, homicide, suicide and deaths from occupational hazards – all made worse by alcohol and other non-medical drugs. These forms of death or damage have important psychological components, depending on personality, early masculine training and experience and expectations, and psychiatric disorders.

From middle adulthood onwards, in the US and UK, married men have a substantially lower morbidity than those who are single, divorced or widowed. Lung cancer, cirrhosis of the liver and diseases associated with malnutrition, are significantly likelier in these three groups. Those with a stable homosexual partner are as vulnerable as the other men without women, quite apart from the advent of HIV infection. Cigarette smoking increases by 300 per cent the likelihood of coronary disease, and men still smoke more than women, although the latter are catching up. In the 1980s the life expectancy for men in the USA, at 67 years, trailed seven years behind that for women – double the difference in

1910. Figures for the UK are similar – about one year longer in each sex. The theory that cardiovascular disease in men is indirectly caused by a Type *A*, workaholic personality, encouraged by ambitious schools, parents and spouses, is losing some of its credibility. Men certainly smoke more and drink more alcohol when working under the stress of competitive business. In Greece and Hungary, where big business is smaller, men show only a 30 per cent excess over women in deaths from heart attack, a tenth of the US score. Perhaps this relates in part to a less ruthless rat race. However, even in Roman Catholic religious institutions, where life is simple and the stresses are similar between the sexes, the sisters outlive the brothers by much the same amount as in the wicked world outside.

Chapter three

Social and learning factors

Even before their baby is born most parents, world-wide, long for a son. In India amniocentesis, the sampling of the fluid bathing the foetus in the womb, has been massively abused. Rather than employing it properly for the detection of important abnormalities and hereditary diseases, its most frequent use has been to check the sex of the unborn child. Between 1978 and 1983, 78,000 female foetuses were aborted – 97 per cent of the total (Pandya 1988). This marked preference for boys is equally fervent throughout the world. It is understandable in agricultural communities from a practical point of view, but the ability to do physical work falls far short of the almost mystical value placed on sons. They are proof of their parents' worth, their immortality. In the west sons carry on the parental name and often their father's business or profession. Grandparents with their feelings for property and family continuity welcome most particularly a grandson. In great families succession side-steps the female to continue the male line.

A wife who presents her husband with a son can bask in the knowledge that she has done the best thing of all. Babies, long before they can understand words, soak up emotions. A male child, especially if planned, must develop a sense of personal worth. Channelling begins – the direct and indirect encouragement of what is seen as appropriate for a boy. From earliest days boys are praised and admired for qualities quite different from those approved for girls. A loud cry, a tight grip, vigorous kicking – all may be perceived as indications of masculinity. Even an obstinate refusal to feed or use a potty may be interpreted as a strong will.

Although boys are, on average, 2 inches longer than girls at birth, they are the less robust sex. Mothers may sense this, or it may be a matter of valuing them more, but boy babies are more often breast-fed and are weaned later than girls. Throughout the period before puberty, girls develop faster than boys, in speech, physically and emotionally. Boys make a massive intellectual and physical advance from around 14, continuing full tilt until 20. They overtake girls, whose development slows to snail speed at 16. Until age 2 there are no obvious differences in behaviour between boys and girls. From 3 to 6 the child becomes aware of his own sex and that of others. Boys are biologically more lively and competitive than girls. These traits are encouraged by parents, who play active games with their sons but talk more with their daughters. Boys may already show marked aggressive tendencies pre-school, and these are likely to continue into teenage – causing trouble. Because of their energy, which is encouraged on the one hand, small boys come in for more punishment than little girls. The quick slap, so easy to do, may also teach that violence is acceptable in an adult.

By age 3, where there is a free choice as at nursery school, boys tend to choose boyish toys, while girls will play with all types until a year or two later. Play differs, too. While girls' games are often a re-run of daily life at home, boys' play is much more imaginative and war-like. It seems that little girls are practising to be adults, but boys are developing their adventurousness and masculinity. It is at the pre-school stage that violence on TV and videos has its most profound effect – mainly on boys. Primary school teachers in the UK are worried to see playground re-enactments of fictional assault – with the children's surprise that real people can be hurt. They do not immediately regenerate like actors and automatons. The 8-year-old boy in the USA who shot dead a 7-year-old girl, using his father's rifle, may have been one such. A minority of middle-class intelligentsia and feminists from all walks energetically treat boys and girls as of identical rather than equal potential. They make active efforts to ban toy guns and tanks – but nowadays the enemy is zapped by lasers, or obliterated from outer space, for which specialized props are unnecessary.

In most families boys are encouraged to 'stand up for themselves' and to be adventurous. If a daughter is tomboyish that is perfectly acceptable, but there is consternation, particularly from his father, if a son shows girlish interests or behaviour. Ninety-five per cent plus of children taken to see a psychologist for sex-inappropriate behaviour are boys. It is funny if a little girl tries to walk in Daddy's big boots. If a young boy does the same in his mother's high heels, no one laughs. There is some justification for this adult unease. While girls with masculine characteristics usually do particularly well academically and

13

show leadership, boys with feminine tendencies are likely to be unhappy at school and to have sexual difficulties later. Female interests in childhood are often the first indication of homosexuality, or more dramatically, transsexualism. The behaviour itself is not responsible for the later developments.

Boys, especially singletons, brought up by a mother alone, lack a masculine model, and are liable to be gentle, domesticated and unconfident. At puberty they may react against their upbringing and become disobedient, perhaps delinquent; some remain lifelong 'mothers' boys'. A boy raised in an all-female environment, for instance, a women's refuge, where men are disapproved of or denigrated, may become insecure, conciliatory and shy, or depressed. The most masculine boys are those who have been well loved and well disciplined, punished more than most and with fathers who are powerful in the family. Girls, by contrast, respond badly to this scenario (Breckenridge and Murphy 1969).

For either sex, place in the family has an important influence. The first-born is always expected to be responsible, more adult, than younger siblings. Girls may be turned into little mothers, but father's, and sometimes mother's, unfulfilled ambitions are centred on their eldest son.

Case: Richard was artistic. His father, a book-keeper, was obsessed with plans for his son to be a chartered accountant. For every Christmas and birthday, for as far back as he could remember, Richard was given books relevant to accountancy. He did not rebel openly but failed every examination and was sacked from every job that his father arranged. Richard made no effort in his marriage either and at 40 is a drifter and a divorcé.

Fathers are of enormous importance in demonstrating to their sons sound values and suitable responses. Mothers are often left with too much of the responsibility of bringing up the children, even in an unbroken marriage. A mother who is emotionally and sexually deprived may unintentionally look to her son for masculine companionship and adult understanding. Widows are notorious for replacing their husbands by their sons, especially the eldest, or only. Sons who are the youngest of several siblings have difficulties of an opposite kind. They tend to be over-protected, indulged and discouraged from growing up.

Deprived children

Boys who are neglected and brutalized as children, develop no feelings of conscience or pity for the weak, and readily become involved in violent crime and sadistic behaviour at home. Those who have been sexually as well as physically abused are a particular danger to others all their lives, sometimes starting as young as 13. Incest, rape and gross indecency forced on females – usually – are commonest in those whose own early experience was equally horrible.

All-male boarding schools, including the most prestigious, aim to toughen up their pupils. They provide opportunities for bullying and sexual exploitation of the younger boys, who may act similarly to their tormentors as they rise in the school. A few are driven into cringing submission at school and unremitting resentment towards others later. Homosexual experimentation at school is usually harmless. Training in the Services can follow the boarding school regime, only more so. There is exhausting exercise, deliberate humiliation and discipline which is usually fair, but may be sadistic if a psychopathic NCO is in charge. The result may be a man who has learned how to suffer without showing it, and how to kill, combined with the idea that authority is his enemy and people are expendable. Women are never trained in this way.

Boys and girls differ in what they value in their teachers. While both sexes rate fairness as the most desirable quality, boys want their teachers to be clever and enthusiastic and girls go for good manners and sympathy. It is stimulus and excitement that engage the interest of boys, while romantic and interpersonal problems pass them by. Part, but by no means all, of this difference between the sexes is due to early channelling and later teaching.

Chapter four

Genetic factors

The glorious sunrise of the science of genetics shone through the second half of the nineteenth century. Hofmeister described dividing chromosomes in 1848, and Mendel worked out the basic rules of inheritance in 1866, using peas. From the 1860s through to the 1890s the deductions of Darwin interlinked with those of Galton, laying the foundations of genetics.

Racial distinctions in bone structure, hair and skin colour were shown to be genetic rather than environmentally determined. Fur-clad Eskimos, living on animal food and enduring cold and long hours of darkness, do not differ substantially from the scantily-clothed, sun-soaked vegetarians of Southern China. Both are short, beardless and of yellowish complexion (Darwin 1871). Differences in temperament and susceptibility to psychiatric disorders are as distinct between races as colour, for instance, the emotionality of Italians, the dourness of Nordics and the extroversion of West Indians. The propensity to guilty feelings and depression among the Jews, alcoholism in the Irish, paranoid states in Poles and manic-depression in the interbred Hutterite sect all show a hereditary bias. The inheritance of intellectual talents fascinated Galton. Gifted families include the Bachs, of whom fifty-seven were musicians; the Wyattes, producing fourteen architects; and the eight mathematical Bernouillis. Criminality associated with kinship was demonstrated by Lange early in this century.

Resemblance of children to their parents is commonplace – a marked difference might raise paternal doubts. Even characteristics that would be thought of as learned, such as 'gait, posture and voice' were noted by Darwin to be recognizable in a man's posthumous child.

Inborn resemblances within races and families are interesting:

genetic differences between the sexes are startling. John Ray in the seventeenth century pointed out the contrast in form and function between a bull and a cow. The sharing of culture, language and religion imparts some similarity between men and women, but there is basic disparity. Women are smaller, by $7^1/_2$ inches in the Javanese, $2^1/_2$ inches among Australian aborigines. Their bodies are built to different designs: the one for childbearing, the other for manual work, whether with a bricklayer's trowel or a bank manager's biro. Genetic and hormonal influences also extend to temperament. Darwin described men as 'more intelligent and aggressive', women as genetically 'more affectionate and self-sacrificing'. Galton, a male chauvinist, saw women as inherently 'coy, capricious and given to deceit' (see Pearson 1914). In the broadest terms, women are constitutionally more verbal than men, men more pro-active.

The mechanics of inheritance

The secret of life lies in deoxyribonucleic acid (DNA). Each huge double helical molecule contains the code for at least a thousand genes. Chromosomes are linear packages of DNA arranged in pairs within the cell nuclei. They are exactly similar in every nucleated cell of the body except the germ cells. Each chromosomal pair consists of two almost identical partners, except for the sex-determining pair. In the female this comprises of two X-chromosomes, but in the male there is a hybrid pair – one X, one Y.

Each new individual receives eleven unpaired autosomes from each parent, an X-chromosome from the mother and either an X or a Y from the father. When the two sex-cells are united the pattern for the future development of the new person is fixed. Mistakes in the instructions, mutations, occur about once per gene per 200,000 years of human life. The risk of a grossly imperfect baby being born is minimal, but detailed individual variations are faithfully reproduced. Genetic defects and disorders may occur in line with Mendelian laws, additive gene effects, or mishaps during meiosis. The latter are likelier after exposure to ionizing radiation, which may break the strands of DNA. Chemicals used to combat cancer may also stimulate mutation. Increasing age acts similarly – Darwin's tenth child, born when his wife was 48, had Down's syndrome.

17

Mendelian inheritance

Genes produce their maximum effects in the homozygote, who has received a similar gene from each parent. Gene effects may be recessive or dominant. In the latter one gene is sufficient to ensure the development of the trait or disorder. Fifty per cent of the children of a case can be expected to show the condition. Onset is often late and the presentation variable, as in Huntington's chorea. The appearance of recessive disorders, such as phenylketonuria, requires a gene for the trait from each parent. Recessive disorders usually reveal themselves in early life. If a gene is carried on the X-chromosome its effects will demonstrate *sex-linkage*: nearly all such traits are recessive. They show little or no sign of their presence in females who carry the faulty gene but also have one normal X-chromosome. The full picture comes out in the male, as, for instance in the Fragile-X syndrome.

Polygenic inheritance

Polygenic inheritance, involving many genes, underlies the genetic aspects of such characteristics as height, intelligence, fertility, longevity – and the predisposition to neurotic reactions.

Multifactorial causation

Multifactorial causation implies polygenic and environmental factors acting together. Having a foster father with a criminal record does not increase the likelihood of criminality in men whose biological fathers were normal in this respect. If the biological father has a record there is some increase in crime among adopted-away sons. If both biological and adoptive fathers are criminal the sons run an enormous risk of being similar. Familial conditions that do not follow Mendelian rules include *semi-continuous traits*, in which the genetic and other factors together have to pass a particular threshold. There may be variations in expressivity and penetrance. Only minor signs and symptoms develop if expressivity is low, while penetrance depends upon threshold. Schizophrenia is thought to be transmitted in this fashion. In sociopathic personality disorders a mild, broad form affects a substantial number of males, but a narrower, more severe form can affect women also (Slater and Cowie 1972).

Chromosomal disorders

Klinefelter's syndrome

This affects only 1 in 700 males. Their karyotype includes one or more extra X-chromosomes: usually 47 (XXY) but occasionally 48 (XXYY) or 49 (XXXYY). The fault is non-disjunction during the first or second meiotic division in the germ cells of either parent. The mother's cells are responsible in 67 per cent, the father's in 33 per cent. There is a sporadic association with older mothers, and with diabetes in either parent. Klinefelter babies tend to be rather small and delicate, but not usually sufficiently to arouse special concern. Until puberty the boy may seem ordinary enough, although behavioural problems are common and 25 per cent show mild mental impairment. Verbal skills are the least affected – possibly due to the beneficial influence of the extra female chromosome. At puberty the development of these cases deviates from the norm. They become tall, long-limbed and eunuchoid in shape, with small testes and minimal secondary sexual characteristics. The voice remains childish and 85 per cent have unwanted breast development. Emotional development is slow, with difficulty in social adjustment frequently paving the path to adolescent delinquency. There is little sexual drive and many are lifelong 'mother's boys' – especially as they are likely to be the last children of older mothers. Submissiveness, inadequacy and dependency are common, with a liability to petty criminality. There is an increased incidence of schizophrenia (Valentine 1969).

Since the presence of the Y-chromosome means that the Klinefelter male has some basic anatomical masculinity, some response may be expected from testosterone injections. Understandably these men often suffer neurotic depression, feeling 'only half a man'. Group and individual psychotherapy or modified bereavement counselling may help (Oyebode and Black 1986).

XYY syndrome

Around 1 in 1,000 males have a 47 (XYY) karyotype. The first case to be described was a tall man of 44, of normal intelligence and with no psychiatric abnormality. He came to notice because several of his children had chromosomal disorders. A hereditary tendency to non-disjunction has been postulated.

Fifty per cent of XYY men are over 6 feet tall, and many have skeletal abnormalities. Nodulocystic acne is common. Levels of testosterone, luteinizing hormone (LH) and follicle-stimulating hormone (FSH) are high, but these are not linked with aggressive propensities (Donovan 1985: 145). There is a 1 per cent likelihood of criminality compared with the norm of 0.1 per cent. In 1968 a man in Melbourne was acquitted of wilful murder on the grounds of his XYY constitution. Since then, however, most courts do not accept the XYY complement as a valid defence in crimes of violence. Mild mental impairment is slightly more frequent in XYY men, but the rarer 48 (XYYY) karyotype is always associated with multiple somatic imperfections and mental retardation.

Fragile-X syndrome

Boys outnumber girls by three to one among the mentally handicapped. This is largely because of a number of X-linked conditions. A third of boys handicapped because of an X-chromosome anomaly have the Fragile-X syndrome: autism is usual, violent outbursts common, and mental impairment severe. The appearance is distinctive: high forehead, big jaw, blue eyes and long 'bat' ears. The testes and hands are large. Inheritance is semidominant and females can only be carriers. Treatment with folate may be helpful in some, but prevention is more important. This is the most prevalent avoidable type of mental handicap after Down's syndrome. High risk families need screening: those in which there is a retarded male, children with autism or large testes. The male foetus of a carrier runs a 50 per cent risk of the disorder (Kinnell 1988).

The androgen-insensitivity syndrome

This occurs in 1 in 60,000 males. It is due to a faulty tfm-gene on the X-chromosome: its role is to organize the development of androgen receptors, of small importance in girls. Males produce much more testosterone than females, and develop accordingly. Androgen-insensitive males – half the sons of carrier mothers – resemble females externally, but have no uterus. Their outlook and interests are feminine, by nature and nurture. Concern is first aroused at puberty by their primary amenorrhoea, and the testes may be located as swellings in the labia or inguinal canals. They are best removed. These 'girls' often become models. They are tall and willowy with feminine breasts and slim hips. They do not lack libido and may marry men happily, although they cannot hope to conceive. Since there is no way of masculinizing these males, it is vital not to disturb their feminine-gender identity and self-image.

Pseudohermaphroditism

This autosomal recessive condition involves the deficiency of an enzyme needed for the production of the potent metabolite, dihydrotestosterone, from testosterone. Until puberty these boys look like girls and are brought up as such, but the pubertal surge of androgens causes them to react by developing male genitalia and the drives and interests to match. The androgenized brain overcomes early learning experiences and the main problem is convincing the parents that their daughters are truly sons. It is understandable that these men are sensitive to criticism and can become neurotic unless treated with warmth and understanding.

Mental impairment syndromes

Sex-chromosome anomalies underlying some forms of mental handicap have been considered. Some rare X-linked conditions also cause mental impairment in males only. *Hunter's syndrome* affects 1 in 40,000 males. It is a type of gargoylism with distortion of bone structure and severe retardation. *Lesch-Nyhan syndrome* (hyperuricaemia) reveals itself in early infancy: motor milestones are missed, growth is stunted, and added to severe retardation is a persistent tendency to self-mutilation.

X-linked hydrocephalus

This is less common than the usual non-genetic form, and mental symptoms are gross.

Other genetically-mediated types of impaired mental development affect males:

Down's syndrome

This is the commonest recognizable form of mental handicap. In 94 per cent the cause is non-disjunction in chromosome 21. The incidence is less than 0.1 per cent if the mother is under 35, rising to 2.5 per cent if she is 45 plus. Three per cent of Down's syndrome subjects have a translocation defect. Parental age is irrelevant for this group: the error may occur as a new mutation or one parent is a carrier. It is usually the mother because sperm bearing an extra load of genetic material seldom reach their target. In Down's syndrome 'everything in the body is a little out of the true' – from head to heart. Both sexes are equally at risk of being born with the syndrome, and for both the maximal mortality is in the first few weeks of life. From 1 to 4 years, however, females have a higher death rate than males. This evens out over a span of sixty years. Down's subjects have small noses with a propensity to upper and lower respiratory disorders. They run an increased risk of myeloid leukaemia and psychiatrically of Alzheimer's disease, developing early. The highest intellectual level in Down's syndrome is about 60 IQ or (Development Quotient) DQ, but the mean is 34 for a male, 39 for a female. Many of these children manage happily enough at nursery school, but they slip progressively further behind their unaffected peers, and few can cope at an ordinary school. As with all handicaps, it is the parents who are likely to suffer most emotionally. It is especially distressing when a son is impaired.

Galactosaemia

In this enzyme deficiency disorder 20 per cent are mentally subnormal, 20 per cent borderline and 60 per cent have an IQ of 90 or more. Most suffer from diarrhoea, vomiting, jaundice, anaemia and later, liver cirrhosis. The condition is ameliorated by a lactose- and galactose-free diet. In the United States 1 in 18,000 is affected, but only 1 in 70,000 in Britain. The disorder appears to be inherited as an autosomal recessive, but twice as many boys as girls are affected.

Cri-du-chat syndrome

This autosomal disorder affects girls preferentially, 3:2. There is mental and physical retardation and a weird cry.

Laurence-Moon-Biedl-Bardet syndrome

This is a recessive autosomal affecting twice as many boys as girls.

Cardinal features are mental impairment, retinitis, pigmentosa, poly-dactyly and obesity.

Autosomal recessively-inherited disorders

These are usually associated with mental retardation affecting the sexes equally, and include Tay-Sachs disease, homocysteinuria, Wilson's disease, Friedreich's ataxia.

Autosomal dominantly-inherited disorders of psychiatric importance

Dystrophia myotonica, Murfan's syndrome, neurofibromatosis, phaeo-chromocytoma, pseudohypoparathyroidism – these five are rare, and affect both sexes equally. More important are acute intermittent porphyria, Huntington's chorea, Pick's disease, Alzheimer's disease and some forms of epilepsy.

Acute intermittent porphyria

This ran through the royal houses of Stuart, Hanover and Prussia and was probably responsible for the mysterious madness of George III. This is an enzyme deficiency leading to attacks of abdominal pain, neuropathy and acute psychosis cropping up at any age. Episodes are precipitated by acute infections, alcohol, barbiturates and methyldopa, and possibly, emotional upset. There is no evidence of preponderance in either sex, but numerous notable men have been affected.

Huntington's chorea

Presentation varies with the age of onset. This can be at any time, but is most frequent in the fourth decade, when unfortunately the victim is likely to have married and had children. The sexes are affected in equal numbers but men, due to their greater tendency to sexual activity and violence, produce more devastating results. An early symptom is disinhibition, leading to inappropriate behaviour. Later there are involuntary movements, progressive muscular weakness, paranoid psychosis and dementia. The responsible gene has been localized to chromosome 4. Other dementing disorders are far commoner but less clearly genetically-mediated.

Alzheimer's disorder

This is a major problem for western civilization. It accounts for 50 per cent of all those diagnosed as demented. Women outnumber men 2–3:1. In Britain there are 570,000 Alzheimer subjects, of whom 30 per cent require long-term care at the cost of £2 billion annually – and increasing. Neuritic plaques, neurofibrillary tangles and neurone loss in several brain areas are characteristic. The cause of the disease is not known, but there are clues. High risk groups include people with Down's syndrome and those with a family history of dementia. Many cases are not obvious until 80 plus, and men in particular may die before this age, which blurs the genetic picture. A genetic locus for early-onset Alzheimer's disease has been found on chromosome 21, that affected in Down's syndrome. On balance it seems probable that there is one form of Alzheimer's disorder mediated through a single gene, affecting the sexes equally, and a polygenic/multifactorial type attacking women preferentially.

Pick's disease

Like Alzheimer's this dementia may come on in the 40s or 50s or the senium. It is seen only a twentieth as frequently, and affects twice as many women as men. There is a gradual onset with loss of social restraint and increasing fatuousness. Male cases arise, on average, a few years earlier than female, and death is similarly earlier: the mean age is 59.5 compared with 63 years for women. Inheritance largely conforms to the pattern of autosomal dominance, but the reason for men being more often spared is not known.

Multi-infarct dementia

This runs in families, but its genetics are inextricably intertwined with those of hypertension.

Epilepsy

This comprises a complex group of disorders. The genes predisposing to petit mal and to febrile convulsions are strongly age-dependent for their expression. The electroencephalographic abnormality underlying absence attacks is inherited as an autosomal dominant only revealing itself at ages 4 to 8 years. Convulsions at a body temperature of 38°C plus occurs in girls from 6 months to 2½ years, in boys from 6 months to 3½ years. The difference is due to a sex-related variation in the timing of neurological development. Severe, frequent episodes of febrile convulsions predispose to temporal lobe epilepsy later. Males in general show twice the incidence of grand mal epilepsy compared with females: largely due to more frequent trauma in men. 'Idiopathic' epilepsy is probably polygenically-transmitted. The risk to a child of either sex who has one epileptic parent is 1 in 40, compared with the norm of 1 in 100.

Personality

Breeding programmes for domestic and laboratory animals recognize the heritability of aspects of temperament. Buckfast bees are the product of years of genetic fine tuning to reduce aggressivity. Maudsley rats have been bred into 'reactive' and 'non-reactive' types. In human families it is generally accepted that children take after their parents in personality – for instance, in having a short fuse or being a worrier. Twin studies show greater concordance in EEGs and galvanic skin responses within monozygotic (MZ) pairs than dizygotic (DZ) pairs.

Questionnaire studies of twins have found that the trait most consistently concordant in MZ compared with DZ twins relates to psychological energy, self-confidence and vigorous activity. On the other hand, degrees of energy differ most widely between the sexes. Extroversion/introversion scores in twins indicate that this trait-continuum is at least 50 per cent heritable. Neuroticism scores, also from the Eysenck Personality Inventory, are more alike in MZ twins than others, but this trait is strongly influenced by circumstances – for instance, it is raised during a period of physical illness. Heritability has been demonstrated in a minority of the scales of the Minnesota Multiphasic Personality Inventory: social introversion, depression, schizophrenia and psychopathic deviation. The last-named is far commoner in males. The California Psychological Inventory shows the heritability of dominance in men exclusively. Unexpectedly, results from twin studies indicate that sharing a common environment – or not – has little relevance to similarities in personality. Conservatism is almost the only feature definitely dependent on the home background.

Personality is important because of its connection with psychiatric disorders, particularly the neuroses. Obsessional neurosis is sometimes regarded as part of a continuum of obsessionality. While the population prevalence of obsessional disorder is 0.05 per cent, first-degree relatives of obsessive-compulsive patients run a 5 to 7 per cent risk of the neurosis, 37 per cent for obsessional personality. Similarly, an anxious personality is particularly frequent among the relatives of those suffering from phobic or other anxiety states, implying a continuum. Alcoholic men are likely to come from families that include others with anxiety disorders.

Antisocial personality (ASP)

This is a disorder in itself, causing harm to the subject and those around him. It correlates markedly with alcoholism, drug abuse and criminality. A Danish adoption study indicates the significance of genetic factors in the development of sociopathy. Nine per cent of the biological fathers of adopted-away sons with ASP were found to have the same problem, in contrast with 2 per cent of fathers of sons who did not show ASP. Fourteen per cent of first-degree biological relatives, of both sexes, of adopted away psychopathic cases suffer from ASP, alcoholism, Briquet-type hysteria or criminality. This is twice the percentage among controls and the adopting families.

There is an interesting and clear link between ASP in men and Briquet's syndrome in women. It appears that for men there is a single threshold above which ASP is obvious, while for women there is a lower threshold for the hysterical disorder than for ASP – on a similar genetic substrate (Cloninger *et al.* 1978).

Criminal behaviour

Juvenile delinquency and minor crime are sometimes considered a *sine qua non* of sociopathic personality, but studies do not bear this out. There is scarcely any difference in the normal prevalence of delinquency and that in youngsters who develop ASP. Genetic factors probably operate in children and adolescents who persist with antisocial behaviour throughout and into adult life; there is no evidence that this group comes from more disturbed or deprived backgrounds. Sex, on the other hand, is highly relevant and men have a markedly lower threshold for developing criminal behaviour. Women are more liable to neurotic, including hysterical, disorders.

Alcoholism and drug abuse

Alcoholism has long been observed to run in families. The biological sons – but not the daughters – of alcoholic fathers or mothers have a high likelihood of alcoholism. It seems almost irrelevant whether or not adoptive parents are alcoholic. Among adoptees with alcoholic parents there is no increase in 'normal' heavy drinking, personality disorder or crime. Alcoholism, depression and ASP are transmitted independently, despite their frequent individual and family association. The great excess of male alcoholics appears to depend largely upon social and environmental influences, and their competence in metabolizing ethanol. Two types of alcoholism are suggested, one comparatively mild, induced by social expectations and pressures, and the other, mainly inherited from father to son, and usually involving serious antisocial activities.

Genetic factors play a key role in the metabolism of alcohol, affecting individual, sexual and racial differences. Many orientals have a comparative lack of hepatic alcohol dehydrogenase, and suffer an Antabuse-like reaction to alcohol, showing, most obviously, in the person's red eyes and face, and can lead to danger of collapse. EEG patterns show similarities in alpha-wave expression among alcoholics: cause or effect?

Drug abuse

As with alcohol, men are more prone to use illegal drugs excessively. Drug abuse and ASP are strongly correlated, and are often associated with ASP in the biological background. Alcoholism in parents is linked with drug abuse in their children. There is also some evidence for a common heritable link between alcohol and opiate dependence. Psychopathology and emotional or social upsets in adoptive families increase the likelihood of drug abuse in vulnerable adoptees (Cadoret *et al.* 1986).

Tobacco

Seventy-four per cent of MZ twins have similar smoking habits, compared with 50 per cent of DZ pairs. Concordance is unaffected by their being reared apart. There is virtually no correlation between the smoking habits of adopted children and those of their adoptive parents or siblings. There is a small correlation between the habits of biological parents and their children. There is still an excess of male smokers, but this is decreasing. Personality traits which have a genetic input precede and predict smoking. High extroversion plus high neuroticism at age 16 are associated with smoking later.

Neuroses

Family studies reveal an excess of neurosis among first-degree relatives of neurotic patients. Neuroses are far commoner in females, but in males there is a stronger genetic component. A polygenic/threshold model would account for the female preponderance, allied to environmental pressures on women and their sex-role stereotype. Severe symptoms, male sex and specific neurosis correlate with a heavy genetic influence. Depressive and hysterical neuroses are more subject to genetic input than anxiety states or obsessional neurosis.

Affective disorders

Family, twin and adoption studies provide consistent, compelling evidence of a heritable contribution to typical, severe affective disorder, either unipolar or bipolar, with some overlap. Genetics are more important in 'endogenous' than neurotic depression. In general, however, there is a 10 to 15 per cent morbidity risk for first-degree relatives of patients with any type of depressive illness. This is somewhat less for men than women, and if the original patient was over 40 at the onset of his first affective illness. A link between depression and HLA-antigens on chromosome 6 has been suggested. In the general population unipolar depressive disorder carries a lifetime expectancy rate of 1 to 3 per cent: four times the likelihood of bipolar disorder. Unipolar disorder is three times more frequent in females, while sexual prevalence is almost equal for bipolar illness.

Bipolar illness is genetically the more important. It has an earlier onset, and first-degree relatives stand twice the risk of illness experienced by relatives in unipolar cases. Early onset of either type is associated with a higher familial incidence. In some families there is evidence of a genetic linkage between bipolar disorder and loci on chromosome 11 and the X-chromosome. Nevertheless, it is unlikely that bipolar illness is X-linked in the majority of cases. There are several well-documented examples of father-to-son transmission.

Schizophrenia

This devastating disorder, expensive in professional care and family suffering, has indubitable hereditary links. Probably two-thirds of the aetiological weighting is genetic. There is a direct correlation between the risk to the individual of developing schizophrenia and the number of close relatives affected. The risk for the relatives of a patient increases according to the severity of his disease. Schizophrenia may be regarded as a continuum from schizotypal personality to catatonic schizophrenia, or as a heterogenous group of disorders, with some caused by trauma or other insults to the brain. Schizophrenics from the same family share – as a rule – the same clinical subtype of the illness. Transmission may be through either parent and does not follow a Mendelian pattern. What is inherited is enhanced liability to the disorder. The polygenic/ multifactorial model remains the most probable, assuming an underlying continuous distribution of liability to schizophrenia. This model presupposes many genes of small effect interacting with a variety of environmental factors and resulting in an overt illness when a critical threshold is passed.

Only a minority of schizophrenics have a schizophrenic parent, but symptom-free parents may each have some of the genes associated with the disorder, but not enough of them, or an insufficiency of the environmental cues for activating the psychosis. The prevalence of schizophrenia in patients' parents is 5.6 per cent, while their offspring run a risk of 12.8 per cent and their siblings 16.7 per cent. The lifetime risk of the illness is approximately equal for both sexes, but the peak incidence is nearly a decade earlier in males. The greater vulnerability of the male brain to early damage as well as differential rates of myelination may be relevant, or this may be another example of differing genetic thresholds between the sexes.

The whole area of heritability in the functional psychoses is confused. Marriages between schizophrenic and manic-depressive partners result in a 17 per cent incidence each of affective psychosis and schizophrenia, but no excess of mixed forms. Schizoaffective disorders seem genetically akin to affective psychosis in some studies, and in others to both manic-depression and schizophrenia. Heston's (1970) famous study on the adopted-away children of schizophrenic mothers showed 10 per cent developing frank schizophrenia, but 26 per cent suffering neurotic personality problems, 18 per cent with sociopathic personalities and 7 per cent having spent time in prison. Eight per cent were mentally impaired and 18 per cent had not married by age 30. Clearly some vague and variable liability to psychiatric symptoms is transmitted. Another facet in the genetic puzzle is the differing prevalence in different racial groups. The lifetime risk is about 1 per cent in Britain, most of Europe and the USA, but in an isolated Swedish community within the Arctic circle, the risk is 2.85 per cent, but there is virtually no manic-depressive illness in the population. In Eire there are proportionately more schizophrenic patients than in any other part of the British Isles (McGuffin 1984).

Chapter five

Aggression and violence

Almost the worst you can say of a man is that he is a wimp: gentle, reasonable, unaggressive – unmasculine. Violence is condemned. Aggression on which it is based is viewed more ambivalently. Disagreement, controversy and competitive striving, fuelled by aggression, are necessary for the development of individuality and to solve common problems. 'Attacking' a problem, 'getting your teeth into it', or even 'slaying' an audience with humour – these are approved. Who could doubt the aggressive approach of Red Adair and his team fighting oil-rig fires, or wish for other than aggressive treatment of a dreaded disease? Righteous anger may be admired; it can certainly be enjoyed. In human relationships sex and aggression are interwoven: the resulting pattern may be marvellously exciting, or brutal. Aggression and fear also intermingle, sometimes leading to appalling acts of violence when criminals get scared.

Beginnings

Assertiveness and aggression develop together up to the age of 3 or 4 years; then they diverge. Similarly boy and girl infants are almost the same in their aggressivity until this age, but from then on boys are consistently more aggressive. In play boys tend to fight for dominance, girls to get their way by guile. Aggression is almost as stable a characteristic as intelligence, and a boy who is markedly aggressive at 4 is likely to be the same at 14. How the characteristic manifests in later life depends mainly on environmental factors: whether he becomes a soldier, a surgeon or a psychopathic criminal.

   In all primates and most other members of the animal kingdom – except for rodents – males are more aggressive than females. The only circumstance in which the female is likely to be fiercer is in defence of her young. There is reasonable evidence that the presence of androgens in sufficient concentration at the appropriate developmental stage induces a masculine pattern of aggression later. Prenatal administration of androgens to female rats and Rhesus monkeys is associated with an unusual amount of rough-and-tumble play postnatally: chasing, threatening, nipping. Boys who are genetically androgen-insensitive tend to be unduly submissive (Chapter 4). Aggressive behaviour increases sharply in boys after puberty, when androgen levels go up. However, there is no consistent correlation between adult testosterone levels and psychological measures of hostility in normal men. Prisoners with a long record of personal violence do have higher androgen readings than control prisoners, but other steroids appear also to be concerned with assaultive behaviour. Another essentially male feature, the Y-chromosome, is associated with violent crime when it is in double supply in the XYY karyotype: but not violence towards other people. Nor are testosterone levels elevated in XYY men (Donovan 1985: 151).

It seems that prenatal androgenization in some way prepares the male brain to react aggressively to certain stimuli, and in the presence of an appreciable amount of sex steroids and degree of muscular development.

Aggressive behaviour varies with age. Pre-school children show a high level – with extravagant threats of killing – which subsides during the early school years. It increases again with puberty and is again slowly reduced during ages 19 to 25. Freud suggested that aggression is a normal drive set off by frustration, and learned in early childhood from the effectiveness in getting mothers to react, of temper tantrums and less dramatic shows of anger. Young chimpanzees have similar tantrums, affecting their mothers similarly.

During childhood girls have a leaning towards looking after younger children, but little boys try to attach themselves to older boys – who stimulate their daring. Among boys, but not girls, there is victimization of any in the peer group who seem 'soft'.

Upbringing that encourages aggression

Adverse factors are parents who are at odds with each other, whose attitudes are rejecting or overindulgent, who do not set reasonable rules and monitor their child's behaviour, and who resort, inconsistently, to threats and physical punishment. Adolescent boys, in particular, are more likely to be aggressive if their early experience is of a negativistic or resentful mother, who accepts violence as the norm. A violent father or stepfather provides a deadly model. Middle-class parents are more likely to reason with their sons than to give them a clip, for control, while manual workers tend to discuss matters only with their daughters. Boys brought up in institutions, although they do not receive physical punishments, develop so little feeling for other people that they have no inhibitions about hurting them.

Television violence has a fascination for young children, especially boys, even though it may make them anxious and disturb their sleep. It is the under-11s who are most susceptible to observation-learning. Eysenck considers that television and videos concerning horror and violence can provoke aggressive behaviour in boys who are socially isolated, culturally disadvantaged and who see a lot of television. Girls are not affected, since all the models – except victims – are male. Subcultural causes of violence extend through adolescence into adult life. Battle on the rugby field allows some boys to test out their courage and masculinity; for others insult, challenge and physical fighting is the cultural style. This is enhanced when adolescents and young adults drink alcohol, diminishing their inhibitions, and go to watch, but have no part in, the ritualized fight on a football field.

While females are aggressive only in response to a perceived threat, particularly involving their child, males show spontaneous aggression, in rivalry, proving themselves as individuals, securing territorial or other rights, and as part of masculine display. Military uniforms are the most impressive and exciting form of clothing, including the ceremonial sword. Aggressive and sadistic phantasies are far more frequent in adolescent and adult men than women. While most men with such phantasies are over-considerate, less demanding than average, those with psychopathic personalities – also likely to be male – may put them into practice.

Abnormal aggression

This lies on a continuum with the normal, and like common law in England, must be assessed by how a reasonable man might behave in the circumstances. In sport it is deplored and sometimes penalized if a tennis player quarrels with the umpire or throws his racket on the ground. It was even worse when a boxer hit the referee: but no one thought of him as mad or criminal. Sportswomen are not immune from displays of pique, but these are mere shadows of the male equivalent. Verbal aggression is a stepping stone towards damage to property, then physical assault. For most people learned inhibitions act as a series of barriers – to obscene language and the various forms of violence.

Violence may be inwardly- or outwardly-directed. The latter may be displaced on to inanimate objects or comprise personal assault, including sexual. Anna Freud considers the causes to be poor impulse control associated with organic brain dysfunction, abnormal defences in psychoses, or ego defects due to poor parenting or a man's efforts to overcome a passive-feminine inclination in himself. More simply, aetiological factors include:

organic problems including trauma, mental handicap, dementia and drugs
schizophrenia
affective psychoses, manic or depressive
neuroses, especially depressive and obsessional
sociopathic personality

Self-harm

This particular form of violence may stop short at a minimal overdose of sleeping tablets, involve self-mutilation, or consist of impulsive violent suicide, or careful planning for a lethal outcome.

Overdosage

Overdosage that disrupts an intolerable situation but does not seriously threaten the patient's life, even in his or her own eyes, is far more frequent in females. The exceptions are children: boys of under 15 are likelier than girls to overdose, and homosexuals with relationship problems. Young women often take overdoses over men; men also take overdoses over men, but not because of women. In general, three times as many females as males make a parasuicidal attempt, and the latter have frequently been drinking heavily. Early loss of the same sex parent, social difficulties and a disordered personality are common antecedents of parasuicide. The major risk of such 'attempts' is repetition with increasing dosage of drugs, and the Russian roulette factor: the person who is expected to find the patient unconscious may be delayed.

Attempted suicide in which the intention was serious but there is failure for an unforeseen reason is far commoner in men. The New Yorker who jumped from the twenty-first floor but was caught by the wind and blown in through a window a few floors down is a case in point. Occasionally drugs like paraquat do not kill either.

Self-mutilation

The commonest type – cutting the wrists or, less often, the legs – occurs in similar cases to overdosage, but the patients tend to even more personality disorder. Females predominate by 3 to 1, but cutters of either sex are usually in their early 20s, married or single, and many are users of illegal drugs, especially oral preparations. Sometimes these patients say that they had wanted to die but more often they explain that someone had annoyed them, or they had become unbearably tense without reason. The cutting itself is usually painless and indeed is felt as a relief. Wrist-cutters frequently suffer from chronic tension, low self-esteem, few internal resources and poor impulse control. The habit of cutting readily becomes chronic, producing thickly scarred arms.

Early life with a sadistically punitive parent leads to the patient's personality being interwoven with strands of sado-masochism, self-denigration, generalized resentment and the linking of love and punishment. Sexual relationships are invariably disturbed. Such patients often demand benzodiazepines, seeing several GPs, but these drugs only make matters worse, relaxing what little control the patient has. Treatment ideally is durable supportive psychotherapy, through crises, dips and disasters.

Mutilation involving eyes or genitals

This is rare, but much less rare in men than women – unlike wrist-cutting. It is usually due to schizophrenic delusions or hallucinatory commands. Depressive psychosis with delusions may also lead to serious mutilation.

> *Case*: a manic-depressive man of 24, recently aware that he had been adopted, became convinced that his blood was tainted with a hereditary disease. He severed his penis to prevent affecting future generations.

Munchausen's syndrome

Munchausen's syndrome, in which the patient may damage himself to simulate illness and obtain admission to hospital, is considered in Chapter 7. It is commoner in men. The patient may sellotape an open safety pin to his back to produce an X-ray picture resembling that if the object had been swallowed; or he may actually swallow a variety of metal utensils, or induce genuine, if mild, haemorrhage from the orifices.

Suicide

At all ages effective suicide is more frequent in males. It is rare before the age of 15, but even then is fivefold commoner in boys. Protective factors in childhood are the low incidence of affective disorder, conceptual immaturity impeding the development of extrapolated despair, and psychosocial support at home and at school. There is a dramatic change after puberty. Among adolescents through to the early 20s the suicide rate has trebled in the last two decades. Suicide is the second most important cause of death for students. Prodromal features in this group differ somewhat from the anxiety and depressive symptoms seen in adults. Social withdrawal, behavioural changes and academic decline should alert concern. Since underlying psychotic illness is more likely to be schizophrenic than an affective disorder in teenage, ideas of reference, hallucinatory voices or delusional ideas may be elicited. Neuroleptic treatment alleviates not only these symptoms but also the associated depression.

> *Case*: the tragedy of Edward Curtis Bennett publicized on television and in the *Sunday Telegraph Magazine* (1988) is typical. He began withdrawing from his friends in his last year at school, and developed overt schizophrenia at 19, suddenly attacking his mother. He killed himself by car exhaust fumes at 22, on weekend leave from hospital.

Over the whole population in both the UK and the USA, suicide accounts for 1 per cent of deaths. In the latter it comes eighth in the leading causes of death. The highest national rate, 25:100,000, occurs in Hungary; the highest rate for any city was in West Berlin; and the highest rate, one a week, for a particular site, applies to the Golden Gate Bridge (Roy 1985). Male suicides outnumber female by 200-400 per cent, and tend to use more violent means: shooting, hanging, jumping, railways. In the USA 50 per cent of male suicides use a gun compared with 25 per cent of females. Self-poisoning is the preferred method for all women in the west, and for both sexes in Britain: probably because of the firearm laws and the familiarity with medical drugs engendered by the National Health Service.

Suicide is responsible for an appalling wastage of male life. Studies indicate that 98 per cent of those who kill themselves are clinically ill, 94 per cent with psychiatric disorders (Robins *et al.* 1959; Barraclough *et al.* 1974). Of the latter, 45 per cent suffer affective illness – indeed 15 per cent of those with uni- or bipolar depression die by suicide. Despite female preponderance in these disorders, the likeliest to commit suicide are male, early in their illness. Twenty-three per cent of suicides are chronic alcoholics – a male-dominated condition. Apart from the direct depressant effect of the alcohol, abuse often leads to such lowering results as loss of employment, financial or legal problems, and family quarrels. The male:female ratio for alcoholic suicide is 4:1. A substantial proportion of alcoholics, about 30 per cent, have a primary depressive illness, and the precipitant to suicide is often the loss of a close relative. In general bereavement, while it induces a feeling that one would welcome death, it does not usually lead to suicide. A chronic depressive mood may arise and in males especially, physical morbidity. Drug abuse, like alcohol excess, is strongly associated with suicide, although it may be difficult to distinguish accidental from deliberate overdosage. The suicide rate for narcotic users in London and New York is twenty times the norm.

Schizophrenia: about 10 per cent of sufferers die by suicide, and there are 20 per cent of those who are not only schizophrenic but have also committed illegal offences. Almost all schizophrenic suicides are male, underlining the greater severity of this psychosis in their sex. As in manic-depressive cases, the patients most at risk of suicide are young men whose illness is relatively recent. Most are in a depressed mood rather than wishing to escape their psychotic symptoms. Twenty-three per cent kill themselves while inpatients, 50 per cent within 3 months of discharge into the community. In Roy's study of schizophrenic suicides (1985), 90 per cent were unmarried, 80 per cent unemployed, and nearly 50 per cent lived alone.

Psychopathic personality disorder, another predominantly male condition, is also associated with an above-average suicide rate: 5 per cent. As with schizophrenia, this is increased threefold if the patient is in prison, or about to be. Neurotic patients in general have a 5 per cent rate, if they are male. Allebeck *et al.* (1988) conducted a vast prospective study, involving 50,465 Swedish conscripts over a period of 13 years. Two hundred and forty-seven committed suicide during the study. Predictive features were poor emotional control; previous contact with child welfare organizations; problems with authority; lack of friends; heavy use of alcohol; intravenous drug abuse. Neurotic illness doubled the risk; personality disorder trebled it. These, of course, were all young men passed fit to serve in the armed services. In the general population the major risk factors for suicide are:

  male sex
  age over 45
  single, separated, divorced or widowed
  isolation
  illness, physical or psychiatric
  uprooted from familiar surroundings
  white race
  unemployed, including retired
  previous suicidal attempt or threat
  in the USA, Protestant religion

Most suicides take place between 6 p.m. and 6 a.m., peaking in particular seasons. In both the UK and Australia there is a sexual differentiation: while female suicides cluster in spring and autumn, males are concentrated in the spring and early summer (Lester and Frank 1988).

Outwardly-directed violence

Deliberate damage to property or to a person, without proper provocation, is similarly motivated in either case: the difference is in degree. Such violence can occur in organic brain states, including intoxication with various chemicals; in functional psychoses; and in neuroses and personality disorders. In all situations, except possibly dementia, male violence outstrips female in amount and seriousness.

Organically-mediated violence

Damage to the frontal, and to a lesser extent the temporal, lobes from any cause – trauma, tumour, atrophy, haemorrhage – impairs judgement and reduces inhibition. Peter Storey (personal communication) describes a man whose extensive subarachnoid haemorrhage involved the anterior cerebral artery. Finding that he had mislaid his key, the patient cheerfully smashed down his front door with an axe. Lishman (1968), studying head injury, found that new development of aggressive and antisocial behaviour was confined to those with penetrating wounds involving the frontal area.

Epilepsy: in general this disorder has a vague, indirect association with violence. Complex partial seizures originating in the frontal or temporal lobes may involve impaired consciousness and automatisms. The latter has been defined by the judge, Lord Goddard, as: 'someone performing acts in a state of unconsciousness'.

Case: a mild-mannered academic of 37 developed attacks of motionless staring, followed by writing reams of rubbish. If interrupted by his colleagues, he would kick and hit them, but have no remembrance of anything unusual. Electroencephalography revealed a left temporal epileptic focus.

This type – temporal lobe epilepsy – is the most likely to be associated with aggression: directed inwards or outwards. Epileptics, particularly those with temporal foci, have five times the usual suicide rate. Aggressive behaviour is most frequent in males, with fits starting early in life, and with a long history of behavioural problems. Fifty per cent of aggressive temporal lobe epileptics are unemployed and many others have low grade jobs and intellectual abilities in the duller range of normal. Epilepsy may be idiopathic – of uncertain origin – or acquired: in a traumatic birth, from meningitis or encephalitis, or after injury in an accident or fight. This latter type of acquired epilepsy is most often associated with inappropriate aggression. These men, of mean age 30, are usually unmarried, again illustrating the beneficial influence of matrimony on the male. Anti-epileptic treatment, if it suppresses the fits, also prevents automatisms, but cannot alter personality traits.

Organic psychoses may be transient, as in delirium or due to drugs, or chronic, as in dementia. Acute organic brain syndromes may follow anaesthesia, the use of hallucinogens, drug withdrawal especially alcohol, or arise with subdural haematoma or in hypoglycaemia from any cause. Such patients may behave with uncharacteristic violence or other bizarre behaviour.

Case: a man of 20 had developed diabetes mellitus at age 11 after finding his father dead on Christmas Day. After puberty he had frequent hypoglycaemic episodes in which he attacked his mother. Glucose deficiency appeared to release aggressive feelings towards his surviving parent which normally were only just suppressed.

Alcohol is well known to relax a man's self-control, so that he may behave with unaccustomed recklessness. In England and Wales, for example, over 40 per cent of murderers have been drinking before the offence, with an even higher percentage in Scotland.

Even apparently calming drugs such as benzodiazepines, and previously barbiturates, have released unexpected personal violence in well-documented cases. This is a physiological rather than a psychotic effect. On the other hand, the combination of alcohol and a hallucinogen or alcohol and Mandrax has been associated with a number of particularly savage murders. Cocaine and amphetamine-like drugs may bring on a paranoid psychosis and the deluded patient, believing himself to be in mortal danger, or doomed, may harm himself or others. Withdrawal from alcohol or barbiturates may operate similarly.

Case: a businessman of 50, in hospital for investigation of gastro-intestinal symptoms, slipped into delirium tremens and waited behind his door with a heavy vase, planning to strike down his doctor whom he believed to be a heavily-armed terrorist. The doctor paused in the doorway and noticed the patient in time.

Sleepwalkers suddenly disturbed and patients in an attack of arteriosclerotic confusion may also hit out, but in a more random, automatic fashion.

Chronic organic brain syndromes: assaultive behaviour may be associated with such brain states as Alzheimer's disease, primary or secondary tumour, multiple sclerosis occasionally, and some cases of mental handicap. It is likely to be directed against whoever is involved in the patient's day-to-day life – often nursing staff or mother. Pathological involvement of the frontal lobes, in whatever disease process, enhances irritability and frank aggression. Among the brain-damaged, children who have had encephalitis lethargica are especially given to violence.

Functional psychiatric disorders and violence

These include depression, mania, schizophrenia, severe personality disorders and neuroses. In depression aggressive feelings are directed towards the self and others who are reciprocally related. For example, murder is followed by suicide in one-third of cases. Such patients – nearly all men – hate those whom they love because they cannot get from them what they crave. They do not show their feelings for fear of losing what they have, however unsatisfactory. Realistic or morbid jealousy accounts for variations on the theme in which a man holds a woman hostage, then kills her and himself.

Divorce or separation can lead to intense hurt and anger, with frustrated love turning to desperate depression. Occasionally a severely depressed man, believing himself to be a failure and the future for his family hopeless, may kill them all before finishing his own life. However, homicidal violence mediated by depression is the one type, apart from infanticide, in which females predominate. The commonest circumstance in which a man harms his - or his girlfriend's - young child is with severe personality disorder, tension and a less important degree of depression.

Mania: violence in manic patients has more nuisance value than forensic significance: among mentally abnormal homicidal offenders less than 1 in 500 is likely to have this disorder. However, violence in those with affective illness is more often personal than directed towards property, in contrast to the situation in schizophrenia.

Schizophrenia: the paranoid schizophrenic projects his own feelings of hostility and self-importance on to the outside world, so that he commonly believes himself to be the target of persecution by a major force – the police, the CIA, interplanetary enemies. Or he may accuse his parents, spouse or colleagues at work of, for instance, poisoning him. Both trivial and serious violent offences are much more often committed by schizophrenics than normals or those suffering from different psychiatric disorders. Males are far more often involved than females. Damage to property is more likely than personal violence and self-harm more frequent than assault. Even among schizophrenics non-psychotic motivation often plays a part. Interestingly, serious personal violence is commoner in those patients who maintain close personal relationships. Murder, when it occurs, usually does so within six months of the patient's discharge from hospital: sometimes too little regard is paid to the relatives' complaints.

While paranoid schizophrenia is so common that it is involved in a large proportion of cases of violence, it is probable that schizo-affective patients and schizophrenics who also have brain damage are the most violence-prone. Paranoid states not amounting to full schizophrenia are also liable to lead to excessive aggression. Morbid jealousy accounts for 10 to 15 per cent of the crimes committed by those in Broadmoor: the hospital for the dangerous criminally-insane. Erotomania which is related to paranoid jealousy, and more common in women than men, underlay the actions of President Reagan's would-be assassin.

Personality disorder

Psychopathic individuals are frequently involved in violent crime. Such people – nearly all male – are likely to suffer defects of both nature and nurture: a mix of genetic susceptibilities and childhood deprivation, with a model of violence, or such gross indulgence that no sense of responsibility or normal values can develop. Characteristically, the psychopath shows a ruthless disregard for the feelings of others or for the truth. Impulse control is scanty, while counting the cost before an action and remorse later are completely lacking. In addition, a paranoid attitude is common and depression not infrequent. Those with a schizoid personality are aloof, superior and craving not only power and importance but love. Their intensely hostile feelings are rigidly contained in such people as Beethoven, Schopenhauer and de Gaulle, but there is a risk that psychosis will break through. The schizoid personality is very much a male type, although some women may be withdrawn and introvert with less hidden hostility.

At Rampton and Moss-Side Hospitals for mentally abnormal offenders, 2 per cent of the patients show abnormalities of their sex hormones, and up to 50 per cent have immature electroencephalograms. Crimes of violence, sex crimes and serious driving offences are often all committed by the same man. Punishment usually only leads to increased aggressivity, since these patients are not afraid of their own or others' hostility. Because of their distorted values they can readily learn to enjoy the exercise of cruelty for its own sake and for the feeling of power. The Moors murderer, Brady, taped the suffering and begging for mercy of his child victims before they died, in this spirit. The multiple murderer Neville Heath was a typical gross psychopath: as a boy he was known as a thief and a liar, showed cruelty to animals and had to leave school for beating a little girl. He grew up into a boastful, plausible con-man and was convicted of posing, at various times, as 'Lord Dudley', a lieutenant-colonel, and another much-decorated officer. Lying, tricking and finally murder for gain were a natural progression (Storr 1968).

While the schizophrenic Sutcliffe killed prostitutes and others under the delusion that he was doing God's will, men of psychopathic and paranoid personality are equally dangerous. Neil, a quiet unsociable clerk, abused and killed numerous young men without being psychotic.

Homicide: the ultimate in personal violence, is – appallingly – the top killer for young men in New York, and the murder rate is sixteen times that in London. This may be largely due to the availability of firearms. Knives are used increasingly in British cities. Women are more often victims in the UK but in neither country are they murderers except under the delusional influence of a puerperal or affective psychosis. Most homicides are unpremeditated, but usually occur during a period of emotional tension – when the means are to hand. Alcohol or other drugs may release the perpetrator from his inhibitions, but in schizophrenic murders alcohol is seldom involved. Fifty per cent of murders take place at night, especially at the weekend, and mostly in the home, and within the family. Wife and children are the most at risk. Among known schizophrenics lethal assaults occur in 0.05 per cent. Most such patients have been ill for more than a year, but may not have active psychotic symptoms at the time of the offence. The homicidal risk in affective psychosis is about one-tenth that in schizophrenia, at 0.006 per cent, also involving those with established illness. A similar risk applies to the severely subnormal, and as in all these disorders, it is the males who are far the likelier to react with violence.

Transcultural aspects: in pre-literate cultures mental illness is not a major factor in homicide. Rather, it is related to infringement of personal space, either physical or social. A high value is placed on physically assertive behaviour in some cultures and subcultures. In the USA it is most admired among American negroes, while in England it is more greatly appreciated by those of West Indian origin than those whose families came from Asian countries.

Amok, in contrast to socio-cultural aggressivity, is a dramatic, culture-bound psychosis, presenting as an acute homicidal form of mania. There is a sudden motor outburst with violent assaults on inanimate objects, animals and people, terminating in exhaustion and amnesia. It crops up in Malaya, Polynesia and the Sahara under various names, and appears to be largely affective in nature.

Psychiatric inpatients: between 7 and 10 per cent of hospitalized psychiatric patients attack the staff. In 61 per cent this amounts to little more than verbal abuse, and serious injury is rare. Among children of 6 to 12 years, boys with conduct disorders are the chief offenders, but among adults sex and race are inconsistently relevant. Age under 40 and a schizophrenic illness increase the likelihood of assaultive behaviour. Alcoholism is the second most frequent diagnosis, but in the age group 65 plus organic brain syndromes top the list.

Neuroses

Neurotic men and women seldom do physical harm to others, although obsessionals may react violently if prevented from completing a ritual. A steward in the Merchant Navy was dismissed from the service for assaulting an officer who had interrupted his complex knife-cleaning procedure. In general, depression, the commonest neurotic disorder, is characterized by severe inhibition of the aggressive drive. The exceptions are those with marital neuroses, comprising a mix of tension, depression and frustration, and often associated with excessive alcohol. Physical violence is implicated in 20 per cent of middle-class divorces, 40 per cent among blue-collar workers. Although women are usually the victims, their role is frequently far from passive. They commonly suffer from low self-esteem and depression, with a childhood experience of neglect rather than violence. Many women report more serious assaults when they are pregnant (Andrews and Brown 1988). The sexual connotations of aggression are emphasized by these cases. More disastrous are 20 per cent of British murders that involve a man killing his wife or cohabitee, and an even higher proportion of 'wife-murders' in America (Home Office 1984; Pynoos and Eth 1985). The most upsetting cases are those in which the child of the woman is witness to the event (Black and Kaplan 1988). These cases, like those of murder followed by suicide (see above) are likely to be committed by men with a psychosis or a psychopathic personality disorder.

Sexual violence: this is practically confined to men, although I know of a sexual assault on a geriatric male patient by a manic female nurse – to the near-disbelief of his relatives. Alcohol often releases inappropriate sexual behaviour, and violence is sometimes the resort of those afraid of sexual failure. Indecent exposure, involving no actual contact, is an offence frequently repeated but rarely leading on to serious sexual attack: the few cases which have culminated in assault occurred when the girl responded to the flasher by laughing. Rapists fall into three main categories: the one-off type where the man may have genuinely misread the woman's reaction; paedophile and the less common gerontophile men, the most psychiatrically-disordered group and the likeliest to repeat similar crimes; and the commonest type, the basically aggressive psychopath, prone to commit a range of violent offences. Sometimes men of schizoid personality cannot ask for the affection they crave, their feelings break through, and they take by force some part of what they desire. In the common, generally violent offender, it is not helpful to employ anti-androgens. The compulsion to exercise power and the gainful aspects of crime are not ameliorated by this treatment. Hormones, anti-androgens and powerful neuroleptics such as benperidol reduce and may control the sexual urge – at the price of some side-effects – but are in no way a cure. Their use by the courts, with the prisoner's consent, evades the issue of treatment.

Child abuse: this includes incest and other sexual and non-sexual non-accidental injury to children. It may be part of general domestic violence: this is surprisingly common, involving 16 per cent of couples annually in the USA, with over a million cases of child abuse. Alcohol and drugs are often part of the scene. There is frequently a violent, alcoholic father or stepfather, or boyfriend, who dominates and bullies his partner. She may collude, for instance with incest, out of fear. In other cases an overtly kind uncle or schoolteacher offers to 'help' a harassed mother by taking her child off her hands for a few hours or putting him or her to bed. Such a man may only look, or touch or photograph the child, and he may be too diffident to approach an adult woman sexually. There is a continuum of self-effacing kindness on the surface with erotic or sadistic fantasies underneath, and frankly sadistic behaviour for pleasure, sometimes involving kidnap. In this range there

45

are a number of men who behave perfectly well until subjected to excessive stress. Such stress may include marital conflict – sometimes no more than sexual deprivation due to the wife's pregnancy – recent unemployment and previous childhood neglect or abuse, prolonged neonatal separation from the child, who in turn may have a difficult personality, and inadequate housing. Girls are more often victims than boys, especially within the family, but paedophilic men are likely to be homosexual.

Idealists, including some feminists, some psychologists and Melanie Klein have envisaged a world in which man's aggressive potential would be so much modified that social interest would supercede human self-interest and co-operation would replace competitive striving – as in the mythological Greek Isles of the Blessed. But the urge to explore and master the environment, including the personal and intellectual, and widespread problems, springs from aggression. Creative achievement in which men have, so far, surpassed women, is related to the aggressive drive. It is well to recall the words of Konrad Lorenz: 'Human behaviour, far from being determined by reason and cultural tradition alone, is still subject to all the laws prevailing in all phylogenetically adapted instinctive behaviour'.

Chapter six

Childhood disorders

Babies differ from one another from the moment they are born – and before, since development begins at conception. It proceeds at an individually variable rate. Sexual differences in temperament are minimal in the neonatal period, but 25 per cent more males die during the first month, indicating their greater physical vulnerability. Regardless of sex, from day one some babies are more reactive and responsive than others: for instance, they are more rapidly soothed after an insult of cold water. Characteristics concerning sociability, emotionality and general activity noticeable at 4 months are still recognizable at 42 months. By 3 to 7 years boys differ profoundly from girls – in aggressivity, which seems to be biological, and in behaviours which are expected and encouraged in sons. Male and female infants with significant scores for minor physical anomalies develop along different lines in the pre-school period. Both have a short attention span, but whereas the girls tend to withdraw socially and are apathetic, the boys are overactive and show aggressive-impulsive behaviour.

Child development is governed by interaction with adults. While intelligent athletic children attract favourable family and outsider responses, those with negative characteristics or any abnormality tend to be scapegoated in times of domestic difficulty. Little boys who react with aggressive behaviour when they are upset receive less sympathy than girls. Separation, loss and disturbed family relationships have a major impact on children – physically, psychologically and behaviourally.

Bereavement

If a parent dies children tend to react, in the short term, with depression, a fall-off in schoolwork, and sometimes bed-wetting. Boys are more severely affected than girls, particularly if it is the father who is dead. Later psychiatric sequelae, for instance, depression in adult life, are most likely if the loss occurred when the child was 3 to 4 years old. Mental illness in a parent has much the same effect on the children as death. The influence of being brought up by one parent alone is considered below.

Divorce

This is more disruptive than death. It commonly occurs in a hotbed of conflict, involving grandparents and friends as well as the two protagonists. A mother left to bring up a child in an atmosphere of harassment rather than support from her husband commonly has less communication with the child, shows him less affection and is less consistent in her control. She may often be distressed, anxious and angry. The least favourable situation is when a mother is struggling alone to bring up a son, especially if she has to start going out to work at the time of the separation, rather than previously, or a year or two later. A girl may identify and sympathize with her mother to some extent, but a boy will often be doubly aggrieved, first, blaming his mother for the loss of his father, and second, for abandoning him herself with her job. This will result in the boy being whiney, disobedient and aggressive, and inclined to ignore his mother.

Boys without fathers, for whatever reason, feel a longing for male company and seek out adult men – even strangers. Indeed boys grow up to be less masculine if no father-figure is available as a model and to play rough games. Older children and teachers are less understanding to boys after parental divorce, because of the way they communicate their upset, yet even two years after the separation, when girls appear to have adjusted well, boys still remain more isolated and have difficulty in making friends. Sad though separation from a parent may be, what is even more damaging to a child is continuing tension and conflict between his parents. This often surrounds access. Boys of 7 to 8 are prone to blame their mothers for the breakup and fear the future loss of both parents. They may become irritable, aggressive, unable or afraid to sleep, and lacking in concentration. While the remarriage of a divorced father often angers the mother and also results in less contact between father and son, if the mother remarries her difficulties are eased, including with her son. Boys of under 9 usually become more settled emotionally with a stepfather in the home. Illegitimate boys brought up by their mothers also benefit in most cases from having a stepfather. Girls are less affected in either situation.

Parenting styles

Quarrelsome and neglectful homes

These produce a high risk of delinquency in boys (McCord 1979) – perhaps because of poor modelling and chancey discipline. Parents who themselves have personality disorders are likely to have sons, but not daughters, who develop conduct disorders, while marital disharmony and maternal depression are associated with behavioural problems even in young children.

Discontinuous care-giving

The type of care that is often provided in institutions may involve as many as fifty different people, mainly women, and many changes. Particularly if this obtains during a child's first two or three years, the development of individual bonds of trust and affection with an adult is impossible. The effect is profound and lasting. Girls so treated feel themselves always inferior, leading to promiscuity and early, disastrous marriages. Boys, by contrast, tend to become thieves, and are unable to form a loving relationship. The pejorative term 'affectionless psychopath' used to be applied to this sad, deprived state.

Overprotection

This is a style of child care in which mothers – predominantly – indulge for their own gratification, in compensation for an unsatisfactory marriage, or because of unresolved, undeserved guilt when a child is sick or handicapped. The result for a son or a daughter may be to encourage the development of any of the neuroses, but not psychotic illness. Sons who become 'mother's boys' suffer social disadvantage: they are disliked and despised by their peers through school onwards.

Over-strict discipline

This does not develop a child's conscience, but produces low self-esteem. This in turn leads to ill-judged behaviour 'to prove himself', or drug abuse and delinquency in a search for peer acceptance.

Lax discipline

This may result from either overindulgence or neglect. Either way it induces aggressive behaviour, especially in boys, which is prone to affect the whole family.

Adoption

In both the UK and the USA adopted children have twice the usual rate of referral to the social and psychiatric services, with an increase towards puberty. Apart from definite disorders affecting the children, it is probable that adoptive parents are readier than others to take their minor problems to the professionals. Emotional and behavioural problems are more frequently reported in adopted children, particularly among boys in the younger age groups, but becoming equal at around 11 years old. Boys, and less often girls, adopted after age 6 show an increased prevalence of stealing and destructiveness. Adopted boys in general are more likely to show signs of maladjustment – fidgetiness, poor concentration and quarrels with other children. Among adult adoptees females, but not males are inclined to develop neuroses. Among the men who were adopted after age 2, alcohol-related problems arise in 16 per cent, while 33 per cent acquire a criminal record. Nevertheless, about two-thirds of adoptees grow up to be reasonably well-adjusted adults.

Fostering

This is the preferred form of care for young children who cannot live with their natural parents. There is a disastrously high failure rate – 50 per cent – making matters worse for those children already maladjusted or emotionally disordered. Boys are more likely than girls to settle badly, particularly if they are more than 4 years old at placement. Difficulties are also frequent with mentally-impaired youngsters. Fostering can be a happy and rewarding experience, however, especially in semi-permanent cases.

Skilled social, educational and psychiatric support to parents, carers and children is needed in all the situations just outlined.

Psychiatric disorders

There is a general tendency for male predominance in childhood psychiatric disorders. They fall into four categories – behavioural, emotional, psychotic and organic, including mental impairment.

Behavioural disorders

These include problems in pre-school children, conduct disorders at any age, and delinquency, bounded by the legal definition for the age of criminal responsibility. Pre-school problems centre on maturational variations and difficulties in establishing acceptable patterns of behaviour with regard to eating, sleeping, sphincter control, socialization and aggression. About 15 per cent of 3-year-old Londoners have some degree of behaviour problem in the ratio boy:girl, 3:2 – the odds lengthen later (Richman 1985). The commonest presentation is a restless, disobedient, attention-seeking child, difficult to control. Boys are more likely than girls to have sphincter problems, overactivity and aggressiveness; while girls more often have fears of the dark, being left, noises or strange objects (see table below).

| | 3-year-old London children | |
	Boys %	Girls %
Bedwetting	44	30
Daywetting	23	8
Soiling	18	11
Restless, aggressive	16	10

Source: Richman 1985

Stuttering – at 4 per cent – is twice as common in boys as girls: it has a genetic as well as a sexual component, since the highest risk is for the male relatives of female stutterers. Aggression, though more severe and persistent in boys, tends to develop earlier in girls.

Although these comparatively minor troubles occur almost as often in pre-school girls as boys, the outlook is worse for the latter. The problems persist in 73 per cent of 8-year-old boys compared with 47 per cent of girls. Similarly, delay in speaking and low scores on early developmental tests are predictive of behavioural and educational difficulties in boys but not girls.

Conduct disorders

These are three times as frequent in 8-year-old boys as girls, although the distribution for emotional disorders is equal. Manifestations include overactivity and aggressive trait disorders: fighting, tantrums, disobedience and destructiveness; antisocial traits: lying, stealing, truancy and wandering.

There is an overlap between the two traits, but the aggressive type is more characteristic of the younger groups, the antisocial type of older children. In boys only there is a correlation between conduct disorder and low IQ, but on the other hand reading retardation in boys is, in itself a cause of antisocial behaviour, through frustration.

Stealing

This occurs in 5 per cent of primary school children, and inevitably involves lying. It is significantly associated with some deprivation of adequate mothering for whatever reason, and is usually a comfort phenomenon in the young, solitary thief. Older boys who steal in twos and threes are often trying to prove their masculinity.

Overactivity and attention deficit disorder

These may occur together, but not inevitably. There is a 'normal' type of hyperactivity which typically arises in a restrictive home with elderly parents. This is in contrast to the relatively rare wild, uncontrollable form in a reckless, impulsive boy – usually from a stormy home with a violent father.

Aggression and impulsiveness which persists through school overlaps with psychopathy. The boy seems heedless of adverse consequences in his pursuit of immediate pleasure. Minimal brain damage, exposure to lead and food additives have all been blamed for hyperactivity on inadequate evidence. Low levels of cerebral serotonin may play a part, however, and there is some indication of a genetic component from adoption studies: involving alcoholism, hysterical and antisocial personality disorders in the natural relatives.

Learning difficulties

While general learning problems occur equally in boys and girls, specific reading disability is three to four times as frequent in boys – probably because of their differential hemispheric development. Twenty-five per cent of children with reading disability also show antisocial conduct. Dyslexia is a related language problem. Later educational failure is usually a failure to use skills rather than a limited capacity, and the causes are motivational, except for – rarely – early schizophrenia.

Fire-setting

This is rare. Eighty-four per cent of fire-raisers are boys, and 80 per cent of the fires are started at home. Peak ages are 8 and 11 years. Less than half the children are living with both their natural parents, and the background is often violent, neglectful and chaotic. Boys tend to react energetically, and fire-raisers are usually also wanderers, destructive and/or soilers.

One-third of boys attending a child guidance centre for a conduct disorder are likely to end up as psychopathic adults: a sociopathic father has a particularly deleterious influence. Behavioural methods of treatment, including the parents if possible, are the most fruitful in non-delinquent conduct disorders.

Delinquency

This is a socio-legal diagnosis applicable to children aged 10 to 17 convicted of what is accounted a crime in an adult. Ninety per cent of cases involve theft, taking and driving away a car, breaking in to steal, and vandalism. Personal violence, sex and drug offences catch public concern but are a small minority. Ten years ago males in the UK ran a lifetime risk of 44 per cent of having a conviction, 22 per cent before the age of 21. The equivalent for females was 15 per cent and 4.7 per cent. The trends are upwards and it is probable that soon it will be a minority of men who are never convicted. Nevertheless, most juvenile delinquents grow out of their habit from about 25. Twenty-five per cent persist in crime. Predisposing factors are deviant parents, a broken home, and living in a neighbourhood where delinquency is the norm. Predictive features are aggressive and anti-authoritarian attitudes at school, truancy, poor educational attainments and being given a bad label.

Moving out of the inner city environment and marriage to a non-delinquent girl are the most helpful developments (West 1985).

Emotional disorders

The so-called neurotic symptoms of early childhood – thumb-sucking, nail-biting, food fads, stammering and bedwetting – are not valid indicators of neurotic or emotional disorders. These involve feelings of inferiority, self-consciousness, social withdrawal, tearfulness, hypersensitivity and persistent sadness. In early and middle childhood boys and girls suffer these equally, but during the teenage years a female preponderance develops which lasts through adulthood.

Anxiety states

Anxiety is commonplace, but excessive anxiety is part of all the emotional disorders of childhood. Infants tend to be afraid of falling, strange people and noises. Later more imaginative fears are common – of the dark, being left, monsters ... From 9 to 12 the main anxieties concern school, friends and money. In adolescence fears centre on bodily injury, disease, sex, failure and 'looking silly'. Boys suffer fewer fears than girls, particularly after puberty. Clinical anxiety states in childhood are often concerned with separation from a key figure, or present as shrinking from all contact with strangers. Some fears are precipitated by, and based upon, environmental stress, such as going into hospital, a new school or an accident. Others develop as a personality trait in association with chronically anxious parents. Parental anxiety is 'catching' and also interferes with the normal parent–child interaction. Support and behavioural techniques are helpful.

Phobias

Animal and insect phobias usually start before the age of 5, and respond well to treatment, with sensible parents. Agoraphobia may start in late childhood, while social phobias begin at or after puberty. See Chapter 7 for details of neuroses.

Hysteria

Hysterical personality, which resembles immaturity in an adult, cannot be diagnosed in children. Conversion hysteria, usually affecting a limb, is uncommon in children, and odd, apparently hysterical behaviour in children frequently turns out to have a neurological basis. Epidemic hysteria, for instance, in schools, seldom affects boys, but individual episodes arise, albeit rarely, in either sex.

Obsessional neurosis

Mild rituals and obsessions are common in children and of no significance, but 0.2-1.2 per cent of children attending a psychiatric clinic have a frank obsessional state. The symptoms commonly start at age 6 to 7 and involve toilet and bedtime behaviour. One-third of adult cases had obsessional symptoms before the age of 15, not necessarily persisting, and in two-thirds the illness began during adolescence. Obsessional symptoms also arise as part of a depressive illness, especially in adolescence, with phobias, and in autism. Boys are more often affected than girls, and the family background is typically middle class with high standards of cleanliness, self-control and morality. Intelligence is likely to be above average.

School refusal

At any one time 10 per cent of children are absent from school. Of these 22 per cent have no legitimate reason. They may have been kept at home by their parents for various matters of convenience; or they may be truanting: part of a conduct disorder; or they may be school refusers. Children in the last group are anxious, neurotically depressed, but basically good and conformist. Boys and girls are affected equally. The onset is usually sudden in younger children, but is insidious and hedged about with physical symptoms in the older group. The problem may be basically separation anxiety, especially in the youngest children, part of anxiety-depression or a phobic manifestation. School, family and intra-psychic factors operate but, although these must all be investigated, it is vital that the problem is dealt with promptly. Behavioural strategies are useful, with either a tricyclic such as clomipramine, or a monoamine-oxidase-inhibitor-type antidepressant if tension or depression are prominent.

School refusers are likely to remain unduly immature and home-bound. Ten per cent of school refusers in Sweden were still living with their parents at 24 to 29 years old, compared with none in a matched control group (Flakierska *et al.* 1988). They also sought psychiatric help more often as adults, and had fewer children of their own. School truants, who are also truants from home, are mainly boys – in contrast to the school refusers, who are fairly balanced in terms of gender – and show other symptoms of conduct disorder.

Tics

The simple type comprises sniffing, throat-clearing, blinking, grimacing or other quick purposeless movements. They can come on any time from 2 to 15 years, but commonly at about 7. Boys are affected three times as often as girls, and there is no association with mental retardation, so it is generally thought that tics are caused by a maturational anomaly to do with neurotransmitter function. Whether or not there is such an underlying susceptibility, tics are quite often precipitated by emotional upsets: serious frights, including rows at home, and acute physical conditions. One-third of the parents of tiqueurs have had some psychiatric problem, particularly depression in the mothers. Simple tics call for simple treatments: reassurance and explanation. They usually improve in adolescence if not earlier.

Gilles de la Tourette's syndrome is a rare and complicated form of tic (see Chapter 7). The sex ratio is the same as for simple tics, but there appears to be a definite genetic factor, with a propensity for Jewish and East European people.

Elective mutism

This term applies to children who can speak but do so only with a few intimates in specific situations, after a period in which they spoke with everyone. Unusually for a speech disorder girls are affected as often as boys. The usual age of onset is 3 to 5, in a child who is shy and sulky, but tends to be aggressive at home. Intelligence is likely to be in the lower 50 per cent of the normal range. Family and behavioural therapy and increasing maturity all help: boys improve more slowly than girls.

Psychotic disorders

Infantile autism

There were isolated case reports of this distressing condition in the nineteenth century, but in 1943 Kanner gave his excellent, definitive description of the clinical features. Boys are affected three times as frequently as girls, but the latter are more severely disturbed, and usually have a family history of cognitive problems. Onset is before 30 months, and affects social and language development. The child tends not to discriminate between parents and strangers, does not make attachments, does not seem to want cuddling, neither follows his mother about like a normal toddler, nor goes to her if he hurts himself. Eye contact is poor, and autistic children do not wave 'bye-bye' or play 'pat-a-cake', nor do they appear to comprehend or use language normally. Their play is stereotyped and they are liable to tantrums and obsessions. Seventy per cent have an IQ below 70, and psychometry demonstrates a genuine cognitive deficit not a motivational problem.

By the age of 5 some autistic children are less grossly impaired, may be friendly to their parents, and enjoy rough-and-tumble play. However, they will have made no friends among other children, have no reciprocal games, no empathy with others. In adolescence normal sexual feelings develop, but it is very rare for them to lead to marriage. Most autistic children end up living in an institution – only 5 to 17 per cent can manage in the community. Fifty per cent gain a useful degree of speech, and half also improve socially, but not as far as normality. About 20 per cent have grand mal fits from adolescence.

This disorder is not a form of schizophrenia and patients do not have hallucinations, delusions or thought disorder. The only significant family history is of language disorders in 15 per cent. Treatment is educational; the parents need support.

Schizoid personality

Asperger's syndrome was described by him in 1944. It occurs almost exclusively in boys. Such children are solitary, friendless, without empathy or humour; they are excessively egocentric, and have unusual interests and attachments to objects, not people. Eye contact and gesture is minimal, but intelligence is not impaired. Most of these cases come from middle-class families and never marry. If there is a connection with schizophrenia it is uncertain and indirect.

Adolescent psychoses

Autism in adolescents shows in lethargy, increased anxiety and tension, and socially embarrassing behaviour, for instance, masturbation or exposure. This type of conduct causes particular concern from a male and neuroleptics are sometimes given to inhibit the undesirable behaviours.

Frank manic-depressive illness is uncommon but of bad prognosis if it arises in adolescence. The symptoms are as in adults, but there are often, also, schizophrenia-like symptoms, including catatonia. Zeitlin (1983) suggests that for practical purposes a single diagnosis of adolescent functional psychosis should be made. Affective symptoms are more frequent in girls, unlike schizophrenic-type symptoms.

Borderline personality disorder

This is not a prelude to schizophrenia, but may cloud the diagnostic issue. It is not the same as schizoid personality (see above) and occurs in either sex. It is thought to result from a failure by the parents in the child's first 2 to 3 years to encourage his independence and autonomy: reminiscent of the outworn theory of 'schizophrenogenic' mothers. Borderline features include intense and fluctuating moods, seriously impaired relationships, apathy and withdrawal or delinquency, depression and transient psychotic episodes. Psychotherapy and help with developing the confidence to become emotionally independent are needed.

Schizophrenic disorders

A large proportion of adolescents who turn out to be schizophrenic were originally given other diagnoses. The best indications are Schneider's first rank symptoms arising in a child who has already seemed isolated within his family, antisocial, and unpopular at school. Florid symptoms do not mean a poor prognosis, nor does a family history of schizophrenia or a disturbed home background. Adverse factors are onset before age 10, insidious development, long-standing abnormalities of personality and such negative symptoms as blunted affect.

Males, under the age of 35, are more often affected than females: see Chapter 9.

Drug-taking

Experiment and ultimate dependence on tobacco or illicit drugs is four times as common among boys as girls. The gap between the sexes over tobacco is decreasing steadily. Regular drug use before age 13 is unusual except for sniffing glue and other inhalants: almost exclusively 9 to 17. While alcohol and tobacco are used mainly socially, marijuana is used in about 6 per cent of teenagers in the UK and USA as a peer group activity, and other drugs – LSD, cocaine, heroin, amphetamines, and so on – are taken because of personal factors. Drug-use, including alcohol and tobacco, by parents, especially the mother, and other models is important; also the relationship with the parents and poor achievement at school. Intelligence is likely to be average or better, but there are a large proportion of educational drop-outs and delinquents. Social class is not directly relevant, but middle-class parents are apt to put more academic pressure on their sons. Girls in a similar situation are likely to react with an eating disorder, rare in males.

Depression

Sadness and tearfulness occur in emotional disorders of childhood and conduct disorders, but clinical depressive illness is rare before puberty. When it does arise the response to tricyclic antidepressants is similar to that in adults. Pre-pubertal boys are as likely to have depressive symptoms as girls but from then the syndrome is increasingly a female preserve.

Suicide

The rate of suicide is increasing in 15 to 19-year-olds but is stable and low before this age, and probably associated with conduct disorder and a disturbed family background. Risk factors are age over 12, male sex (five times the female incidence), disciplinary crisis, family history of major psychiatric illness, superior intelligence, truancy or school refusal. The increase in suicides from 15 affects males predominantly, and is part of an increase in young adults (see Chapter 5). Parasuicide, mainly by overdosage, in contrast to genuine suicide, often using violent means, is commoner among female adolescents, as among young adults.

Cross-gender behaviour in children

Even among young children, masculine behaviour is acceptable in girls but feminine ways cause anxiety and ridicule in boys. Apart from parental concern, feminine boys tend to be alienated during childhood.

Transsexuals are three times likelier to be males. Most of them liked little girls as playmates and preferred girls' toys and clothes. In such cases the child may have been 'delicate' and very beautiful, and have been encouraged by his mother to dress up and make up; fathers withdraw in such circumstances.

Transvestites and two-thirds of homosexuals say that they were effeminate boys (Green *et al.* 1987). Homosexuality is twice as common in men as women. Although homosexuality is less of a handicap nowadays, transsexuals and transvestites suffer considerable social distress as adults. It seems reasonable to help little boys to enjoy their masculinity and to foster it – it is so greatly valued by society. Fathers or surrogates need encouragement to play their major role with male children.

Sexual abuse

This is a particular cause of public concern. Fifteen per cent of victims are boys of average age 11, in peaks at 10 and 14. The likeliest abusers are family acquaintances, then fathers and stepfathers. While the worst long-term effect of such abuse on girls is for them to become prostitutes, boys are more likely to identify with the perpetrator and repeat his deviant behaviour. Family and individual therapy is of the utmost importance for present and future.

Physical abuse and neglect

Either boys or girls may be the victims but, again, violence to a young boy makes it more likely that he will, as an adult, be violent to children.

Boys are physically and psychiatrically more vulnerable than girls. Because of their biological propensity for taking action – a side effect of aggressivity – boys are apt to cause greater family, school and social repercussions when they are disturbed. This characteristic develops during toddlerdom and continues throughout life. At puberty male and female diverge still further, the former longing for risk and excitement, the latter seeking security and affection. Delinquency, drug abuse and suicide are male preserves, while females predominate in eating disorders.

Chapter seven

Neuroses

The very word 'neurotic' conjures up the image of a tiresome, over-emotional female. Helgason (1964) found the lifetime prevalence of neurosis in Iceland to be 9 per cent for men, 17 per cent for women: this applied particularly to depressive, anxiety and aesthenic states, but not to obsessional neurosis. For the latter the sex distribution is even (Black 1974). With this exception, it may seem at first glance that women have a near monopoly of neurotic disorders, yet one-third of the medical casualties among American servicemen in the Second World War were due to 'combat fatigue', 'war neurosis' and other neuropsychiatric problems. Individuals of either sex, developed from the fusion of a male and a female germ cell, comprise elements of each character. Men, because of their asymmetrical cerebral organization, have less inherent capacity for verbalization and self-expression. Their early training teaches them to suppress any display of fear, pain or sorrow, or even love and sympathy – which women can show without shame. When normal emotions of anxiety and sadness overflow into neurosis, it is usual for female patients to present as unhappy, afraid and angry. Their male counterparts suppress their natural feelings, including aggression, so that they erupt in unpredictable outbursts of irritation or silent moodiness – and in some individuals apparently motiveless antisocial behaviour. Doctors compound the situation by a reluctance to categorize their male patients as neurotically anxious or depressed, making it even more difficult for them to reveal such negative feelings. Physical symptoms are far more acceptable.

Dysthymic disorder, as defined in DSM III, refers to a neurotic type of chronic depressive mood, short of depressive illness. The sufferer overreacts to normal and other stresses, and complains of inability to enjoy anything: 'nothing interests me'. Despite his own low self-esteem he is demanding and critical of others, often blaming them for his dissatisfaction. Patients of this type are difficult to treat since they 'do not feel up to' co-operating with manoeuvres which might be expected to result in an improvement. They try the easy options: more cigarettes and alcohol, more food, anxiolytics (anti-anxiety medicines), holidays and health farms: none is effective. Because the term has only recently come into use, the prevalence of dysthymic disorder is not known: it is probably somewhat more frequent in women (Reus 1984). The familiar 'difficult' and continually disgruntled husbands and fathers come into the category. Their families live round their moods in reflected misery. Medication is usually unhelpful, while individual sessions are exhausting to the psychotherapist, yielding little result. Nevertheless, it is worthwhile if the patient can be led to express verbally his half-repressed resentments towards key figures in his life. Group therapy helps these men to interact more honestly with other people, and find self-respect and respect for them.

Depression

This most common of all psychiatric complaints ranges from evanescent sadness and lowering of vitality, through tormenting self-denigration and despair, still basically reactive and neurotic, to genetically-determined depressive psychoses. Major depression, as delineated in DSM III, covers the whole spectrum, but in this chapter affective psychosis is specifically excluded. International classification of disease, edition 9 (ICD 9), defines neurotic depression as 'disproportionate depression which has usually recognizably ensued on a distressing experience . . . anxiety is also frequently present'.

Whichever way depression is regarded, women have more of it. The current prevalence of major depression in the USA is 3 per cent for men, 4 to 9 per cent for women. In London, in a study based on eight general practice groups, twice as many females as males suffered neurotic depression. McGuffin and his colleagues (1988) found the risk for depression among first-degree relatives of depressed probands (the original case whose children, parents etc. may or may not have the disease) to be 23.5 per cent for women compared with only 8 per cent for men. Flor-Henry (1983) considers the female brain to be far more vulnerable to all types of affective disturbance because of its relatively weaker organization in the non-dominant hemisphere – lacking the influence of androgens. (The male organizational pattern, by contrast, increases the risks of autism, schizoid personality and psychopathy.) There remain unexplained anomalies, for example, the more severe the depression the less the female excess, and among those over 60 the sex ratio is unity. While more women are diagnosed as depressed, proportionately more men are referred to specialists, and there is a small, statistically insignificant, preponderance of males admitted to hospital. These disparities between the sexes may be due in part to men playing down their symptoms until they are so marked that the patient is incapable of carrying on at work. The stigma of a psychiatric diagnosis and the inconvenience of being unable to function in the outside world are taken less seriously for women.

While men do not readily admit to emotional distress in words, they may manifest it in other ways: as delinquency in juveniles, psychopathic behaviour in young men, overuse of alcohol and illegal drugs, and in the older groups painful and other psychosomatic complaints. It is significant that in the large Scandinavian and London studies of depression, which show such an excess of females, cases involving alcohol abuse are excluded. Another anomaly from McGuffin and his colleagues' study was a striking difference in life events. Men had fewer events than women during the two months preceding the onset of neurotic depression. While mild life events ran at a generally lower level for men than women in this period, they increased in similar proportion and with the same timing. Serious life events were less frequent before depression for men, compared with women, and there was a longer time-lag between event and symptoms. It seems that many of those who succumb to neurotic or reactive depression are particularly susceptible to stressful experience. Protective features against the slings and arrows are male sex, paid employment, financial security, age under 50 – and for men only, marriage, especially if the wife stays at home. It is interesting that married women are much more likely to be depressed than married men, and it makes matters worse if the husband is at home. Even an apparently longed-for retirement often turns out to be a major stress on both parties.

Unemployment

This may be a complex life event or a chronic difficulty. Jobless teenagers of both sexes score highly on psychometric measures for depression and anxiety (Warr 1982). Among adults males are the more severely affected and risk factors include age over 50, unemployment for over a year, high level of work involvement previously, and poor domestic back-up. Depression is the commonest reaction, and exacerbation of somatic complaints, particularly gastrointestinal disorders, asthma and psoriasis. Parasuicide is closely associated with unemployment, according to Platt and Dyer (1987).

Bereavement

While on the whole men are less likely to become clinically depressed in response to domestic disasters, loss of a wife may be literally lethal. Spouse and children occupy far more of a woman's time and concern than a man's and her life-style and emotional equilibrium are more upset by deaths, disappointments and changes in the family. The loss of a baby in this century of low infant mortality causes incapacitating grief for the mother, while depression is also frequent in the mothers of handicapped children. Fathers, whose life is less directly affected, seldom break down with these strains. Even after the loss of a spouse the initial reaction seems much more severe in women: with more weeping and overt distress, and a greater need for psychotropic medication to attain self-control. Throughout the first few months of bereavement widows express more bitterness and anger than men and are more likely to continue breaking into tears when discussing their loss. Men, by contrast, say that they find the pain and grief diminishing by the third month, and they are more willing than widows to consider the possibility of remarriage. These differences may be 'macho' or in part due to the very different treatment accorded to newly 'available' men in our culture, compared with widows. Bereaved men, including divorcés, are given a great deal of practical help and support from female friends and neighbours. Widows are more commonplace, and as women are expected to cook and keep house for themselves.

However much better men seem to cope – emotionally – with bereavement in the short term, by twelve months the degree of upset is similar among widows and widowers. At follow-up two to four years later, it appears that it is the men who take the longest to recover completely (Parkes 1981). More sinister is the increased death rate, especially from heart disease, in men recently widowed. In the study by Young and his colleagues, later confirmed by Parkes, the mortality rate for widowers was found to be 40 per cent higher than for married men of the same age during the first six months after bereavement. It remained above the norm for four years. Widows also tend to more illness after their loss, but not to statistical significance. Unless there has been an unusual one-to-one relationship, men take the death of their parents in their stride, showing no increase in physical or psychiatric morbidity, and indeed are far less emotionally upset by the death of any relative but the wife. The manifestations of normal grief are the same for both sexes:

a process of realization, ranging through disbelief and numbness
an alarm reaction, with restlessness and insomnia
an urge to search for the dead person – in some form – in familiar places
anger and guilt, often expressed in resentment towards helpers
a feeling of internal loss or damage
identification phenomena: the symptoms, phrases or mannerisms of the dead person are reproduced
recovery, a new start in life, in a different role

Pathological grief

Freud's paradigm of depression is a prolonged, often delayed reaction, with insomnia, lack of energy, weight loss, sadness, anger and guilt, and inability to enjoy anything. This amounts to neurotic depression with bereavement the precipitating life event. Men are more likely to succumb if they had been forced into the role of chief provider of care during the wife's or partner's terminal illness. For this reason, and also because less neighbourly and family sympathy and support is forth-coming, bereaved homosexual men fare particularly bleakly. This is likely to be an increasing problem, with deaths from AIDS becoming more frequent. In these cases there is the added fear – or reality – of having contracted the infection: at least some counselling services are available, voluntary and as part of the hospital provision.

Loss of a limb

Because of greater exposure in dangerous occupations, sport and road traffic accidents, men are more likely than women to lose a limb. The reaction is analogous to that after the loss of a key person and goes through much the same stages. Bitterness and envy towards healthy, intact people is frequent, with marked loss of self-esteem, similar to the plight of widows whose social role is devalued dramatically with their changed status.

Treatment of neurotic depression

The somewhat different presentation in men must be borne in mind when planning management in depression. Increases in alcohol and tobacco consumption are more prominent in depressed men than women, so that delayed rather than initial insomnia is common. Lowered libido and impotence, aggravated by alcohol, are particularly damaging to a man's self-opinion. Irritability and inefficiency at work also matter more to men, and make a miserable situation worse. Suicidal risk is greater in men and they are more likely than women to use violent – and immediately effective – means. Although suicide more often occurs in manic-depressive, than neurotically-depressed men, from middle age onwards, there has been increasing concern in Australia from 1987 about the number of young men shooting themselves. Aside from these impulsive acts, which are difficult to predict and prevent, factors which should arouse especial vigilance in treating a depressed man include social isolation, alcohol excess, physical illness and feelings of guilt. Appreciable suicidal risk in reactive depression calls for close supportive contact and ready availability by the therapist, and continual reassurance about the patient's worth as an individual. A minority of cases require hospitalization.

The prime ingredient in helping all reactively depressed patients is supportive psychotherapy, one-to-one, and in some cases group work also, after the initial stages of recovery. Warmth and empathy need to be spiced with encouragement to positive thought and action, including involvement with other people. Cognitive therapy is a variant based on Beck's concept (1979) that faulty thinking, often becoming habitual, drives the depression. Adjustment by logical steps into a less maladaptive mode is achieved by frequent, regular sessions, and 'homework' set by the therapist aimed at improving by achievement the patient's self-image. 'Guided mourning' comprises taking the subject, willy-nilly, through the reality of his loss – of wife, job, familiar home, or health – and his own feelings, however negative, stage by stage. Day hospital attendance is useful for men unable to work yet or without a job to go to, particularly if they live alone or in a hostel. More chronic cases can move on from the day hospital to a day centre or a sheltered workshop. For men it is essential that they feel that they are contributing something in a practical way, whereas female patients may be content with discussion groups, classes in self-care, yoga and relaxation: occupational therapy that is not like work.

Medication

This may be useful in a minority of cases, especially for those whose depression has developed on a substratum of chronic tension. Mono-amine oxidase inhibitors (MAOI), such as tranylcypromine (often best given in combination with trifluoperazine as Parstelin) or phenelzine, are usually the most effective. Male patients need clear warnings about strong cheeses, red wine and lager, as well as the other incompatibles: meat and yeast extracts, pickled herrings, over-the-counter cold cures and other drugs. MAOIs have the disconcerting side-effect in some men of inducing impotence or delayed ejaculation: such effects require explanation, reassurance and a reduction of dosage if possible. Tricyclics are less likely to be helpful in neurotic depression, and in older men care must be taken not to precipitate acute retention. Half the standard dosage is appropriate for the over-65s. The newer drugs (mianserin, maprotiline and trazodone) are sometimes useful, parti-cularly if insomnia is a problem. Fluvoxamine is not yet established as completely safe and effective.

Anxiety states

Everyone is anxious some of the time – survival depends upon alertness to danger. Thus, manifestations of anxiety are commonplace – emotional tension and apprehension, and the somatic results of beta-adrenergic autonomic discharge. These include dry mouth, tachycardia, raised blood pressure, pallor and sweating of the skin, increased visceral muscle tension, and more rapid breathing. Somatic symptoms develop if anxiety is excessive, undischarged or sustained. Mowrer (1939) suggested that anxiety is a learned response to threatening signals, and acts as a drive towards escape behaviour. The threat of an imminent viva voce examination lies in the possibility of failure and induces serious revising in advance, and when the time for this is past, such well-known symptoms as urinary frequency. Men, especially, are afraid of failure – in work, examinations, sexual performance or courage. Unlike women, success enhances their popularity with the opposite sex.

Anxiety may be part of, or secondary to, various syndromes, both psychiatric and physical. It is usually an integral factor in depression, and is always present in the neurotic type and in the other neuroses – hysterical and obsessional. Schizophrenics are frequently perplexed, plainly anxious or quite terrified in response to their hallucinations and delusions, although they may seen oddly unmoved by realistic threats. Alcohol excess and drug abuse, particularly benzodiazepines and cannabis, are often inextricably interwoven with anxiety symptoms, making withdrawal difficult. Hallucinogens, such as LSD, and stimulants such as amphetamine, may cause anxiety.

Physical disorders directly leading to anxiety include hyperthyroidism, phaechromocytoma, the aura of temporal lobe epilepsy, hypoglycaemia, some acute organic brain syndromes and the onset of dementing disorders. Primary clinical anxiety presents in two forms – free-floating, in which the patient has psychiatric or somatic symptoms but does not fully recognize their origin, and phobic anxiety. In this type the patient knows exactly what object or situation he fears (but not necessarily any inner meaning) and he realizes that his anxiety is excessive compared with that of other people.

Anxiety neuroses

This is particularly frequent in western culture. In the UK, USA and Sweden the estimated prevalence in the general population is 2 to 4.7 per cent and 10 to 14 per cent in patients with cardiac disease, mainly men. Apart from this group it is young adults who are most often affected. The sex distribution is equal for severe anxiety neuroses, but for patients not considered ill enough to warrant referral to a hospital clinic, two-thirds are women. Acute anxiety symptoms may last from minutes to days, and may range from restless unease to stark panic of uncertain cause. One type of anxiety neurosis – panic disorder – comprises recurrent panic attacks; in another there is a milder, more chronic state. As well as apprehension, psychological symptoms may include irritability, restlessness, poor concentration, incoherence even to the degree of being unable to say a word, fear of going mad or being rooted to the spot. Depersonalization, and less commonly derealization, are peculiarly unpleasant. Somatic symptoms, frequently interpreted as indicative of physical disease, may add to the patient's anxiety, for instance, dizziness, faintness, sweating, tremor, tension-related pain in neck, chest or abdomen, nausea, shortness of breath, diarrhoea and frequency of micturition, palpitations. Hyperventilation, a symptom of anxiety, may induce a cluster of alarming physiological effects such as carpopedal spasm, paraesthesiae, fits, muscular spasms, tachycardia and palpitations, and altered states of consciousness. Men are especially prone to jump to the conclusion that they are having a heart attack.

Initial insomnia and weight loss may also be presenting features of anxiety neurosis. Whichever symptoms predominate, the patient will be unable to function effectively in his work, social and sexual life.

Treatment

Analytical and supportive psychotherapy yield disappointing results, but a course of anxiety management training sessions may be moderately helpful. Positive self-statements and relaxation ploys are the basis. Men are apt to try their favourite medication, alcohol, and it brings the same temporary relief as do benzodiazepines, which are more favoured by women. Neither is curative and their use makes it more difficult for the patient to respond effectively to psychotherapy. They both have an addictive potential, and 60 per cent of alcoholics started drinking because of anxiety symptoms. Buspirone is a new non-sedating, non-benzodiazepine anxiolytic. Unfortunately, most patients prefer lorazepam or diazepam. Monoamine oxidase inhibitors (MAOI), sedating tricyclics or major tranquillizers in low dosage, may help the chronically tense patient and are not habit-forming.

Phobic states

Specific fears, exaggerated and leading to avoidance or panic may occur as a phobic disorder *per se*, or – like general anxiety – may arise in the context of a depressive illness, alcohol or drug dependence, obsessional neurosis or schizophrenia.

Childhood phobias affect boys and girls equally. They are particularly common in regard to separation from a parent or the approach of a stranger. Animal phobias are most likely to appear from 2 to 5 years, school phobia from 5 to 16. Among adolescents social phobia is the most frequent – 40 per cent of the victims are male.

Adult phobics are more than twice as likely to be women as men if they suffer from agoraphobia, the commonest incapacitating form, or if they fear an animal. Fears of injury, illness or death affect the sexes approximately equally, but for realistic reasons men are more likely to have a phobia concerning AIDS. Herpes genitalis phobia affects both sexes.

By far the most effective treatment is behavioural, with desensitization in imagination or *in vivo*, maximal exposure, modelling, and in some cases social skills training. Drug therapy is indicated when the symptoms are part of a depressive illness – phenelzine, an MAOI, or clomipramine, a tricyclic, are the most useful but are extremely dangerous if given together, or within two weeks of each other. Anxiolytics are useful for isolated events, for instance, in flying phobia if there is no time to desensitize.

Battle-related phobias or battle anxiety mainly affect men. Combat fatigue, war neurosis, and in the First World War 'effort syndrome' can scarcely be termed phobic since they centre on genuinely lethal situations, but they are incapacitating through purely psychological mechanisms. Rapid treatment and return to the feared situation works better than a prolonged rest in a safe place.

Obsessional neurosis

This rarest of neuroses accounts for 1.5 to 3 per cent of adult psychiatric cases. There are regional variations, for instance, admissions for obsessive-compulsive disorder in Eire are 2.8 times as frequent as in England and 3.3 times as frequent as in Scotland. Over 70 per cent of cases had shown immature or obsessional personality traits pre-morbidly, but such traits are anyway common. They are found in 14 per cent of the US population. Obsessional symptoms, as opposed to the pure neurosis, may arise *de novo* during a depressive illness, in association with agoraphobia, after encephalitis, particularly encephalitis lethargica, and following trauma to any part of the brain. They are characteristic of some epileptic patients.

Despite the frequent concomitance of obsessional symptoms and depressive illness, there is no genetic link. Both neurotic and psychotic depressions are commoner in women, whereas obsessional neurosis is equally distributed. Obsessional behaviour with its connotations of magic is commonplace among children of either sex, but the neurosis is rare, usually coming on suddenly after the age of 7. Peak incidence is in the early 20s – less than 15 per cent begin past 35. Obsessive-compulsive neurosis may consist of obsessional ruminations – horrifying, disgusting, sexual, or philosophical, or of compulsive rituals. These include hand-washing, touching, counting and complex dressing routines. Mild symptoms may be more or less concealed by the patient, so that the only overt signs are irritating slowness at work, because of checking, indecisiveness and lack of flexibility. Any changes outside

71

the subject's control can precipitate an exacerbation of symptoms, for instance, a new office, different lighting or a new colleague.

Severe obsessional neurosis is more crippling than schizophrenia, and is particularly troublesome in men. If attempts are made to cut short their rituals their aggressive tension may result in physical violence, causing relationship and legal problems. Obsessive-compulsive behaviour in the sexual sphere can also have unfortunate effects – few girlfriends will tolerate a man who keeps them waiting for hours, because of checking his dressing, or insists on certain rituals in his love-making. If an obsessional accidentally brushes against someone in a public place, he may feel compelled to touch him or her again, often an even number of times – an activity that may be misinterpreted.

Mild cases respond to behavioural measures – response prevention and modelling – and, for ruminations – satiation and thought-stopping techniques. Medication, particularly clomipramine, and ECT are most helpful in cases involving depression. Among severe primary cases only one-third make an adequate recovery, making this the neurosis of worst prognosis (Greer and Cawley 1966). It is one of the few diseases for which psychosurgery is considered a viable option. A small minority of obsessional neurotics later develop a schizophreniform disorder.

Gilles de la Tourette syndrome

This rare and bizarre disorder includes some obsessional features. It is significantly more prevalent in males. Usually appearing before the age of 16, it is characterized by multiple motor tics and compulsive shouting. Early on this is a wordless noise but it may progress to a string of obscenities. A monochrome edition is the sudden, unfulfilled impulse a normal person may have to say something shocking out loud in a church or other solemn assembly. A non-specific organic component to the aetiology is likely and accords with the association of obsessional symptoms with cerebral lesions. Butyrophenones such as haloperidol, clonidine, behavioural methods such as massed practice, and increasing personal maturity alleviate what may otherwise be a lifelong handicap.

Hysteria

From its very name, hysteria has been historically associated with the female sex. Sydenham, in the seventeenth century, recognized that men suffered from an equivalent disorder, hypochondriasis. Robert Whytt

(1768) developed this theme, but in the nineteenth century Landouzy (1846) placed hysterical symptoms firmly in the feminine context. They required: 'Youth, warm climate, springtime, civilized society, hereditary disposition and menstrual irregularity'. Many of Freud's patients were women with hysterical neuroses but men were not, and are not, immune. Hypochondriasis as it is now understood is not a male equivalent of hysteria, but hysterical phenomena in men often present differently from the stereotype.

Hysterical personality

Hysterical personality, involving theatricality, manipulativeness, suggestibility and an immature outlook on life and sexuality is more frequently found in females, partly because of cultural expectations and early training. However, unlike the situation with obsessionals, the personality is not significantly linked with the neurosis.

Hysterical neurosis

This comprises conversion or dissociation phenomena and the somewhat separate Briquet's syndrome which, alone, is genetically-mediated. Conversion and dissociation symptoms usually occur in adolescents and young adults and serve the same purpose – to provide an immediate escape from an acutely anxiety-provoking situation. There may also be secondary gain. Sexual problems and anxieties commonly lead to a hysterical reaction – the music-hall jokes about headaches that militate against marital relations demonstrate an appreciation of hysterical mechanisms. Men often complain, more obviously, of penile pain when the thought of intercourse is alarming, or unpalatable.

Hysterical amnesia

This involves loss of personal memory but not of skills and general information, for instance, how to read or what cigarettes and lighters are for. The contents of the patient's purse or pockets are oddly uninformative, unlike the situation in organic amnesia. In the latter the patient is likely to be old, drunk or drugged, confused or obviously ill. Hysterical amnesia in women is most commonly connected with sexual indiscretion – a schoolgirl or wife who has had an adventure she cannot explain, on the way home. In men it is far more often bound up with absence without leave, broken bail or other legal difficulties. In a fugue the patient wanders away from home in a state of amnesia, nevertheless managing to obtain food and look after him or herself.

Multiple personality

This goes a step beyond hysterical amnesia. It was regularly reported at the turn of the century – encouraged by medical interest. Some cases were merely prolonged fugues, in which a secondary name and life-style were imposed on the patient by circumstances, for instance, the wretchedly married vicar who left home and established a new identity over some years, having forgotten his earlier life. Almost all truly alternating personalities have been women, however. The notorious American multiple murderer, Bianchi, used the defence of two – or three – personalities and deceived several psychiatrists until finally shown to be an ingenious psychopath. In genuine cases time, mild sedation and reassuring explanation are curative – hypnosis may induce further dissociation.

Combat hysteria

This has affected servicemen of all races, including French, Russian, Indian, British and German. In the First World War it reached epidemic proportions. Conditions for the combatants were dreadful and the casualty rate for servicemen considerably higher than in the Second World War, when civilians were also under attack. Illness in the first war meant honourable escape from an appalling and dangerous existence. Social attitudes and the physicians' failure to understand their patients were conducive to the development of physical symptoms. The conditions described were soldier's heart, effort syndrome or neurasthenia, all three with breathlessness, fatigue, palpitations and precordial pain.

Shell-shock – originally thought to be due to cerebral and spinal concussion, but observed to be oddly contagious. It manifested in initial confusion and excitement, then irritability, emotional liability, and any of the hysterical symptoms described among soldiers at the time: aphonia, stammering, wrist-drop, foot-drop, deafness, blindness, blepharospasm, tremors, jerks, fits, paraplegia, headaches, nightmares, insomnia, depression. When psychiatric treatment was finally used – sedation, abreaction, encouragement and rapid return to the line – there was a high cure rate. By the Second World War military medicine was well able to manage such cases.

Of 1,000 combat hysterics in the North African campaign, only fifty-four were ultimately invalided out. Nevertheless, even now 8 per cent of military patients with closed head injuries develop conversion symptoms at some stage in their recovery (Merskey 1979). The degree of cultural sophistication influences the types of symptom. Abse (1966) compared the hysterical symptoms of British and Indian soldiers, respectively. The former suffered mainly headaches and other pains and paraesthesiae and 10 per cent were amnesic. Among the latter fits were by far the commonest symptom, then abdominal pain, and in 25 per cent, amnesia.

Epidemic hysteria

In the west, in the last thirty years, outbreaks of hysterical illness have nearly all affected schoolgirls and young women in closed communities. Males have been scarcely at all affected. However, pop festivals, with the addition of drugs, induce a degree of mass dissociation, temporarily, and some mainly American-based religious or pseudoreligious cults influence young men as well as women. Techniques have been used, for instance in the Rajneesh cult, to induce abnormal suggestibility and thence abnormal and sometimes dangerous behaviour.

Briquet's syndrome (somatization disorder)

This involves a dramatic and complicated medical history with at least twenty-five chronic and recurrent somatic symptoms, beginning before age 35, and with little objective cause. Monosymptomatic conversion hysteria resembles Briquet's syndrome in all but its scope – complicating factors in both include drug dependence, parasuicide and marital failure. Unlike the single symptom complaint, Briquet's syndrome is practically confined to women, and there is a substantial genetic component. The male relatives of Briquet patients show an excess of sociopathy and alcoholism. Similarly, male criminals who develop conversion symptoms are more likely than others to show manifestations of psychopathic personality, alcoholism, drug addiction, parasuicide and previous admission to a psychiatric hospital.

While hysterical illness is by no means confined to women, except for the Briquet type, and adolescents and young adults of either sex may be affected, in middle age there is a definite female preponderance. It may be significant that hysterical symptoms are frequently encountered in Klinefelter's syndrome, in which the male has an extra X-chromosome and has a mildly submissive personality.

Munchausen's syndrome

This comprises factitious or simulated illness, backed up by a dramatic, fictitious account of personal tragedy. The most severe cases are usually men, wandering from hospital to hospital, often inflicting quite marked self-injury in their efforts to produce physical signs.

> *Case*: Colin, C., 32, has produced apparent haemoptyses and haematuria and other physical effects for some years, but has recently moved to psychiatric Munchausen – with symptoms of suicidal depression and a story of his girlfriend's recent death (she is particularly upset by this). He drinks excessively but irregularly, abuses benzodiazepines, and is an opportunist thief. Years of psychotherapeutic care, help with housing, jobs and money – none has produced any improvement.

Like most Munchausens, Colin had a loveless childhood. This disorder 'demands' care and attention which is soon rejected. Male Munchausen patients are especially aggressive. Dermatitis artefacta, in which the patient excoriates or otherwise damages his skin, while denying any such thing, is a limited form of Munchausen, equally difficult to treat. Women have this type as often as men.

Pathological lying is a concomitant of Munchausen's disorder, or it may occur without artefactual illness. The underlying psychopathology is similar, and again the most florid cases are usually male.

Self-harm, such as wrist-cutting, cigarette burns and non-lethal overdosage is often a related disorder with a hysterical basis. Women outnumber men, however, 3:1. Sado-masochistic fantasies, often associated with childhood experiences, may be brought out during psychotherapy.

The Ganser syndrome

This rare disorder was first described by Ganser (1898) among male prisoners, but can also arise in women under stressful conditions. The cardinal features are:

vorbeireden – nearly correct answers to questions
clouding of consciousness, often apathetic
somatic conversion symptoms, especially ataxia
visual or auditory pseudohallucinations.

This is sometimes called a hysterical dementia, but while it is partially a dissociative disorder, depressive symptoms frequently persist when the Ganser features have gone. Unlike Munchausen's and the self-harm syndromes, there is no flavour of sociopathy in the Ganser patients.

The couvade syndrome

Pregnancy is a stress on the mental equilibrium of both parents and may renew earlier psychological conflicts. Psychogenically-based physical symptoms occur in about 1 per cent of expectant fathers, but gross symptomatology, interfering with the man's life and amounting to the couvade syndrome, is rare. It is recognized among servicemen, usually manifest in abdominal discomfort, vomiting or increased appetite, or there may be toothache or other pain. The most attractive explanation is empathy with a deeply-loved partner, but couvade case marriages are not particularly close or happy. The stimulus to sexual and aggressive drives induced by the woman's pregnancy may lead to internal conflictual tension. In couvade cases this is resolved by somatization. No treatment is necessary.

Hypochondriasis

This time-hallowed term used to apply to the male equivalent of hysteria. By analogy to the latter's association with 'movements of the uterus', hypochondriasis was thought to be based on physical problems in the digestive organs. The definition gradually evolved and is now 'a mental preoccupation with a suppositious physical disorder: with a gross discrepancy between the degree of preoccupation and the grounds for it'. Merskey (1979) divides hypochondriasis into 4 types:

1 A delusional part of a functional psychosis.
2 A symptom secondary to dementia or an organic condition.
3 A hysterical manifestation with conversion symptoms and a relative absence of fear of disease.
4 Pure hypochondriasis, with conversions, and much anxiety and concern about health.

The last two, neurotic types of hypochondriasis, are both difficult to recognize. Pure hypochondriasis has a male preponderance; it occurs in rigid, insecure and falsely assertive personalities. They are self-centred and pedantic, and covertly dependent on wife or mother. Common background features are being the only or youngest child, closeness to a dominant mother, and athleticism when young. Treatment for pure hypochondriasis is unsatisfactory since the patient's life revolves round his 'disease'. For instance, an insurance executive planned his day's work to be always within reach of an accident and emergency department that would perform an immediate electrocardiogram. He had 550 in ten years. His cardiac fears were based on his wife's genuine attack of myocardial infarction, from which she recovered well.

Pilowsky's (1978) concept of illness behaviour in hypochondriasis leads to behavioural management. This rewards the patient for non-invalid-like behaviour and allows him the clear choice between keeping his illness status or trying to cope with it.

Chapter 8

Eating disorders

Eating disorders comprise anorexia nervosa, deviant eating associated with work, like that of a jockey or dancer, bulimia nervosa and obesity. They are all more prevalent in females.

Anorexia nervosa

This neurotic disorder is about eighteen times commoner in girls than boys, but presents similarly whichever sex. The essentials are a wilful refusal to eat enough to maintain a normal weight, marked loss of weight, and a lack of interest in sex, usually in a conscientious, hard-studying adolescent from the middle class. Parents are likely to have high academic expectations of their child, and there are underlying family tensions which are never discussed openly. The rejection of food is based on a fear of taking on adult responsibilities as portrayed by the parents, but this is not readily admitted.

The first description of a male anorexic was made by Richard Morton (1694) about a minister's son who was studying too hard, just as today when anorexia nervosa most frequently arises in the run-up to GCSE or A-level examinations. The minister's son was noted to have no physical disease to account for his wasting away. He recovered on removal from home and a milky diet – much as might be advised now. Whytt (1767) described a boy of 14 who refused to eat, but after losing weight switched to compulsive overeating – bulimia. Boys, like girls, may be affected prepubertally or at any stage of adulthood, although the greatest prevalence is from 15 to 20. Among the male cases there is an absent or feeble father in 25 per cent, rather more than with girl patients. Malcolm is 16 and has recovered his lost weight and returned to school, but he has not spoken to his mother for four months. Langdon-Brown (1931) observed this hostility to the mother in his male patients. Most anorexic boys are of normal height, but two cases which developed prepubertally stand out as having stunted their growth dietetically. In each case this was by something more than simply cutting down on 'fattening' foods. Charles, 11, refused to eat anything but peanuts and raisins, and even induced his boarding prep school to fall in with his wishes. His mother had married twice and had an older son from her first marriage, towards whom she was particularly protective. Charles attracted a great deal of her concern and attention by his diet. Adam was a thoughtful intelligent boy who deliberately chose a diet of Chelsea buns to limit his growth so that at 15 his bones were like those of an 11-year-old, the age at which he started to diet. The safety and privileges of being as small as a child were of value to him. Margo (1987) found several of his patients were short.

Treatment has not advanced in the last thirty years, and depends still on inducing the boy to eat and restore his body weight, concentrating on simple, easily-absorbed foods rather than rich dishes. During and long after the weight restoration phase there must be discussion and encouragement towards independence and assertiveness in the face of parental and other pressures. This is likely to be needed over a period of two years or more. In young patients who develop the disorder before age 18, a few family discussion sessions are helpful. Family communication is usually poor.

The main reasons why anorexia nervosa is so rare in boys is their less alarming puberty, with no menarche, no deposition of fat over hips and thighs, and the absence of the social obsession with thinness current among females in western culture. Not many adolescent males aim to be small, thin and frail-looking (Dally and Gomez 1979).

Occupational weight control and exercise

Male racing jockeys usually start serious training at 15 to 16 years. From then on they have to keep their weight down during the season – summer. They use various manoeuvres: appetite suppressants, periods of near-starvation, laxatives, diuretics and saunas (King and Mezey 1987). Binging in reaction to severe restriction is common, but vomiting to get rid of the food is rare in these young men, unlike the situation in bulimia nervosa. Jockeys usually achieve a weight loss of about 13 per cent, but sometimes reach a loss of as much as 21 per cent of their body-weight. Libido is reduced during the season. However, psychologically there is no resemblance to anorexia nervosa among jockeys: they show none of the depression commonly accompanying anorexia, have no distortion of body image, and no fear of fatness, or relevant family conflicts. In winter they happily restore their weight to normal.

Other mainly professional sportsmen may also try to manipulate their body-weight and composition. Boxers sometimes need to lose weight urgently and do it by getting rid of fluid. More serious and damaging is the reverse situation when athletes want to build their bodies up, specifically the muscles. The testosterone-related anabolic steroids are a tempting but officially forbidden ploy – if a doctor can be induced to co-operate. These drugs are variably effective, but at the long-term cost of liver damage, even tumour, jaundice, high blood pressure and water-logging, cramps and headache.

Compulsive jogging and other exercise is more frequent in men than women. Men who want to tone up or slim down do not go in for half measures like yoga and cutting out sweets. They often decide to achieve fat loss by energetic work-outs and persistent exercise. Whether they have started jogging to lose weight, ward off ageing, or just for pleasure, in a minority it becomes an obsession. When this occurs it is likely to be because of endorphin production. Excessive exercise is a type of stress that induces the brain to manufacture extra supplies of its own narcotics, the endorphins – not as powerful as heroin, but similar. The addictive exerciser enjoys and continually tries for more of his home-made endorphin 'high'. Apart from the immense amount of time used up by the compulsive activity, and the consequent damage to relationships, there are also physical hazards. In the short term a heart attack may be precipitated – as in the fatal case of America's most famous jogger, Jim Fixx. In the longer term traumatic fractures and later arthritis are likely to affect feet, ankles, knees and hips.

Bulimia nervosa

Bulimia nervosa may develop out of anorexia nervosa or arise *de novo* in an adolescent or young man. The essence is a chaotic diet with overeating binges matched with self-induced vomiting and/or laxative abuse, alternating with periods of severe food restriction. The vomiting may be so frequent that the enamel and then the dentine of the teeth is dissolved away, and laxatives may be taken by the dozen. Weight may be normal, high or low. The least effective of these weight-control manoeuvres is the use of laxatives, since little but fluid and minerals is lost. Male bulimics usually have over-close but ambivalent relationships with their mothers and their girlfriends or wives. The ambivalence towards these women sooner or later develops into frank hostility, and treatment involves helping the patient to escape from his dependency. There may be an increased likelihood of homosexuality among bulimic patients (Robinson and Holden 1986). Apart from supporting them while they reorganize their unsatisfactory relationships, it is essential to guide bulimics out of the harmful habits of vomiting and laxative abuse. A spell in hospital may be needed to retrain chaotic eating practices and build a better life-style.

Obesity

Although men have less propensity to put on surplus fat and less anguish over shape than women, fatness is far more dangerous for the male. The risks depend on where in the body the fat is sited, and this in turn depends on the sex hormones. Girls, when they hit teenage, lay down fat over their hips and thighs. Fat women tend to be pear-shaped, stalk uppermost. Boys in adolescence, by contrast, slim down over the hips and develop muscle – not fat – over their broadening shoulders and upper trunk. The muscles have a small amount of fat over them as a fuel reserve. In general, men have less fat than women just under the skin except for one small area – the nape of the neck. This is a protection to the spine if heavy loads are carried – commonplace in the Third World only. After about age 70 the fat distribution is similar between the sexes. Meanwhile, when men become fat they become apple-shaped rather than pears. Their fat concentrates above the navel and when it is excessive there is typically a sharply jutting upper abdomen, with the waistband of the trousers slung below the bulge. The waist is wider than the hips.

A man's abdominal fat, instead of lying subcutaneously, is packed inside the abdomen, under the muscular wall. This is where the danger lies. In periods of excitement, emotional and some physical stress, fat is released into the bloodstream, to provide the muscles with extra fuel if physical action, such as fighting, is required. Of course, in the modern arena, muscle power is seldom what is required, and the liquid fat remains unused in the blood. It may stick to the blood vessel walls, clogging them. This can lead to a rise in blood pressure, thrombosis and heart attack. Fat men are more at risk than fat women for two reasons.

Fat under the skin and over the hips and thighs – as in females – is mobilized only slowly, a trickle in the bloodstream. Fat inside the abdomen – as in males – is released rapidly, flooding into the blood. Second, while women's less efficient muscles can run on fat, men have more of the fast-acting muscle fibres which use only glucose. While women may be obese and suffer few problems except wear and tear on their joints, for men the same degree of obesity can be a health hazard and shorten life.

The main reasons for adult men putting on weight are social and related to success. A car for transport and television for entertainment affect all who can afford them, and machines have cut down drastically the call for physical effort at work. Career success means not only less muscular work, but more celebratory and 'working' lunches and dinners, and meals at home, with the likelihood of richer foods, washed down with wine. Alcohol has a specific fat-sparing property so that, whatever the drinker chooses, his liver is likely to be overloaded with fat. The 'beer belly' is well known, but there could equally be a Chianti abdomen.

Men who were very active in sport at school or as young men cannot keep up to the same standard from their mid-30s – and in team games are no longer included. Less muscular activity means that much less nutrition can be used up, and the muscle mass is readily replaced with fat: the man may not realize his change in body composition for some time.

In childhood and adolescence, obesity in a boy is largely a parental responsibility. A long illness, prolonged incapacity from an accident, or handicap – anything inhibiting natural lively activity – is likely to lead to putting on weight, unless less than a normal diet is provided. A child who is deprived of adequate parental time and care may be fobbed off with sweets, crisps and TV; if he is lonely he may overeat for comfort. If another sibling outshines one son academically or is otherwise particularly approved by his father, it is an understandable reaction for his mother to serve the 'unlucky', unsuccessful boy the biggest portions, plus extra treats. This can have a double disastrous result: by making him a 'fatty', which leads to rejection by peers, and by teaching him that being loved equates with feeling full of sweet foods. The fate of a child fat through adolescence is unfortunate. The likelihood of lifelong obesity is much greater than if he puts on weight in adulthood.

Dieting, distraction and exercise are the planks by which to achieve a normal weight, so important for a man. Most men are unmoved by appeals by their loved ones or dire warnings from their doctors: much as applies to alcoholics. Similarly, fat men will sometimes make Herculean efforts only for their work: if this can be shown to be in jeopardy there is a good chance of their cutting down.

Chapter nine

Psychoses

Psychosis is the most serious type of mental disease: madness, in lay terms. Characteristic of psychosis is more or less intermittent loss of contact with reality, which is replaced by the thoughts and imaginings of the patient's own disturbed mind. The psychoses comprise those in which the brain is structurally intact but its working impaired – the functional type, and those in which there is a physical fault or lesion – the organic type.

Functional psychoses

Schizophrenia

This is the most important of the functional psychoses both in the devastation it causes to the individual and his family and its economic consequences. The huge mental hospitals were built to contain and to provide asylum predominantly for schizophrenics. The currently developing network of hostels, day centres and community psychiatric nursing is also largely absorbed by patients disabled by schizophrenia. The prisons also house a proportion of them and the homeless wanderers of the inner cities – nearly all men – are 50 per cent schizophrenic. Delusions and hallucinations are the most striking symptoms of psychosis. Because he cannot distinguish fact from his personal fantasies, the psychotic may act on the latter, in a way that appears unpredictable. Psychotic women are often noisy and verbal but men, because of their greater propensity for action, are likely to react to their false beliefs with antisocial or dangerously violent behaviour. It can range from feeble striking out with his stick by an Alzheimer sufferer, to cunning and brutal killing by a deluded young schizophrenic.

By no means all schizophrenia results in florid symptoms. There is a very different type, arising out of the acute illness or developing *de novo*, in which the illness manifests in negative symptoms: withdrawal from active and interactive life, with loss of initiative, basic social skills and routine self-care. In neither case can the patient be left to fend for himself. The way in which a tendency to schizophrenia may be inherited is gradually being unravelled. The relevant genes can be transmitted through either parent, but an interesting quirk has emerged.

A gene in the autosomal part of the sex chromosomes leads to children of the same sex developing schizophrenia, only if their father carries the gene. Inheritance through the mother may affect children of both sexes (Crow *et al.* 1989) Schizophrenia is by no means a simple matter of heredity. The most intractable cases often arise in a healthy family. After a difficult birth or trauma soon after – a time of intense brain development – there is an increased risk of schizophrenia later. A head injury in later childhood, particularly affecting the left side, may also set the scene for the early appearance of the disorder. It may begin to reveal itself in adolescence, when the brain is vulnerable from the shedding of supernumerary neural cells. There is a slightly higher risk for those born in the early spring, whichever sex or country.

Males develop schizophrenia almost a decade younger than females: perhaps because the brains of the former are more susceptible to early damage, the left hemisphere is less developed or there is a lower genetic threshold to the disease in the male. Of children attending a child guidance clinic in New York, a little over half are boys and two-thirds of these become schizophrenic. Boys who are to become schizophrenic tend to have phobic, obsessional or free-floating anxiety symptoms, whereas girls have no prodromal pattern. Irishmen who drink heavily are more likely to develop schizophrenia, and men – but not women – of Caribbean origin are about four times as likely to become schizophrenic as others, either in the UK or the West Indies. Men who develop schizophrenia are less likely than women to have a major life event as a precipitant; in fact they are likely to have had a particularly uneventful period preceding the onset of the disorder.

Reviewing first admissions to hospital for schizophrenia – at 25, 70 per cent are male; at 35 the numbers are equal, and from 55 onwards there are two to three times as many women as men presenting. Only 15 per cent of late paraphrenics are male: this is a dilute form, in which the personality is unimpaired. The outlook is more ominous for men with an early onset psychosis: remissions are less complete and exacerbations more severe. Partly because their illness comes on sooner, fewer schizo-phrenic men than women marry – 30 per cent compared with 70 per cent. Divorce is common, again much more so for the men. Fertility is reduced for both sexes, but sexual activity may be frequent. Odd perversions are not unusual for the males, and intercourse is unrelated to affection or tenderness. Some of the antischizophrenic medication may damp down both emotion and desire.

About 50 per cent of schizophrenics live at home, with parents or spouse, but within this 50 per cent only 20 per cent are male. A few live with their children, but none of these are men. In the inner cities there are three times as many patients, nearly all men, with no supportive relative or friend. Homeless, rootless, hopeless men provide the largest proportion in cardboard city: living under the bridges, on railway stations and in doorways. Many are alcoholic as well as schizophrenic, drinking anything from scrumpy to meths (Tomison and Cook 1987). Of the lucky ones at home, while two-thirds of the women are supported by their husbands, over half the men are cared for by their mothers. Less than a third have a job. The rest use their time unproductively, with a tiny minority sporadically attending a day centre. It is a relief for the family if the patient is out part of the day, and this is particularly true when there are children at home.

The problems the caring relatives have to contend with include the patient's social withdrawal in 90 per cent, odd, embarrassing behaviour in 60 per cent, and in fewer than 30 per cent violent or threatening behaviour – but much more alarming in a man. Florid symptoms remain largely suppressed if medication is taken meticulously, but periodic relapse is to be expected, particularly if there is some disturbing change or event, such as bereavement. Parents find it more tolerable to have a schizophrenic daughter at home than a son, so the latter is likely to be in hospital more often and for longer. On discharge, men attend less regularly as outpatients and make a poorer social, sexual and occupational adjustment in the community than women (Salokangas 1983). Very few wish to return to hospital, however.

Mothers naturally feel responsible for their children of any age, either sex, and are protective towards schizophrenic daughters who are mildly ill. They often feel unable to control, or actually afraid of their sons. Fathers identify with their sons, and while they can accept a schizophrenic daughter, find the negative symptoms – passivity, lack of initiative, dependency – of a son particularly unacceptable.

Schizophrenia is a life-wrecking disease, worse in every way for men than women: nevertheless, there have been men of great talent who were still able to do wonderful, sensitive work after they became ill. Richard Dadd the painter, and John Ogden the pianist and composer are two such.

Affective psychoses

Disorders of mood, including psychoses, are at least twice as frequent in females as males. Affective illness presents in two widely contrasting forms. In depression the victim feels empty, hopeless, worthless or worse: harmful to others. He/she scarcely eats, sleeps or performs the normal activities of living. Suicide is common. Mania, the other affective psychosis, manifests in overactivity, racing thoughts and speech, boastfulness beyond reality, impatience and irritability. In older patients there is often a mixed affective state with anger and tearfulness together, and an agitated restlessness. In manic-depressive illness of the bipolar type episodes of depression or of mania arise at different times, sometimes alternating. Either the manic or the depressive episodes may be the more severe. In unipolar illness there is either recurrent depression – or uncommonly, recurrent mania.

In men the rate for manic-depressive illness is 8-10 per 100,000, with peak incidence at 55 to 64 years. For women the figures are 15 to 20 per 100,000, peaking at 60 to 69. The original onset for either sex is usually at age 30 to 40 years, but patients who are predominantly manic often develop the disease earlier. Rather similarly to schizophrenia, men are likely to suffer a more serious and disabling illness. Since they often have the manic type, it not only comes on earlier, but the episodes are more frequent and last longer. In only 23 per cent of manic depression in which depression is the major component are men affected, but it is almost evens when depression and mania rate equally, and when mania predominates 62 per cent of the patients are male (Belmaker and van Praag 1980).

While men run only half the risk of recurrent depression compared with women, when they do suffer psychotic depression suicide is a major danger. The incidence of suicide in men increases inexorably with age, up to and beyond 85. Unipolar mania is uncommon, and almost always confined to males. The differences between the sexes in the features of affective psychoses relate to differing brain hemisphere organization. In mania and bipolar illness there is increased metabolism on the left side, less well developed in the male. In schizophrenia, by contrast, both hemispheres are affected, with reduced metabolism. There are other divergent factors in depression between men and women. While life events and lack of support are important in triggering depression in women, for men they have only a 3 per cent influence. Men seem most affected by damage to their sense of personal competence, and depression is relatively rare during the main, well-established working period of 45 to 64. It increases sharply during the next decade. Retirement is one factor, but physical impairment is even more important. Thirty per cent of depressed older men have some physical disorder. Marriage appears to have an ameliorating effect on the risk of depression in men only. Treatment with medication is the same for both sexes, but in middle-aged men the tricyclic anti-depressants like amitriptyline may precipitate urinary retention. Trazodone, fluoxetine and mianserin do not have this anticholinergic effect. Lithium is valuable prophylactically but some creative men consider it hampers the flow of originality. Neuroleptics are even more necessary for manic men than women, temporarily.

Even more than with schizophrenia, many famous men – and women – have had manic-depressive illness: Martin Luther, Hemingway, Faraday, Poincaré. Some like Van Gogh died by suicide in a down phase.

Schizoaffective psychoses

These combine cyclical mood swings as in manic-depression with florid schizophrenic symptoms, but not the negative type. Delusions, hallucinations and thought interference may occur. There are two types: schizodepressive and schizomanic, the former responding to anti-depressants and lithium, the latter to neuroleptics. Schizoaffective disorder seems distinct genetically from the two major functional psychoses, and shows a marked female preponderance – only 28 per cent are male. Two factors which confound the issue are the propensity for women with manic-depressive illness to develop schizophrenic symptoms over the years, and the increasing liability of elderly men to depressive psychosis.

Organic psychoses

There are two main categories, acute and chronic.

Acute organic reactions

These may result from almost any cerebral upset – injury, infection, endocrine or metabolic upset, vascular incident, tumour or abscess, after a fit, and drug toxicity. The symptoms are mainly non-specific, with impaired consciousness, worsening at nightfall, and jumbled memory. Usually the patient is inactive, but in delirium tremens – commoner in men – noisy and excited behaviour accompanies disturbed thoughts and perceptions. Head injury is an underlying cause of an acute brain reaction more often seen in men, but thyroid disorders more often affect women. Acute reactions may subside over a matter of days, or be the forerunner of a chronic organic state.

Wernicke's encephalopathy, characterized by the sudden onset of mental confusion, staggering gait and nystagmus, results from thiamine deficiency. It most often occurs in alcoholics – usually male – and is made worse by the direct toxic effect of alcohol on the brain cells. It is liable to leave the patient with a Korsakoff psychosis, permanently. Immediate treatment with intravenous thiamine is mandatory.

Delirium tremens is an alcohol withdrawal syndrome, popularly known as 'the horrors', and like all alcohol-related disorders, commoner in men. Standard physical withdrawal symptoms accompany mis-interpretations and visual and auditory hallucinations. One victim attacked the telephone flex with a stick, thinking it to be a snake. Long-term alcoholic brain damage may follow, particularly if there is more than one attack of DTs.

Chronic organic syndromes

Some, including Korsakoff's psychosis, are non-progressive – the result of limited damage. In other cases general deterioration can set in on the heels of an acute state, or a primary degenerative process may arise, as in Alzheimer's disease. Hospital admissions for dementia in the elderly exceed admissions for all other psychoses put together – an enormous and increasing social and economic problem.

Alzheimer's disease occurs in two forms – senile in the over-65s, and pre-senile. The far commoner senile type has a multifactorial origin, including a small hereditary input. Aluminium has been blamed and there is an increased risk for those with Down's syndrome, immune deficiency disorders, Hodgkin's disease and, in women, thyroid disorders. It is two to three times more frequent in women, with an average age of onset of 75, compared with 73 for men. Patients are usually dead within five to seven years, and men in particular rarely last longer.

Onset before age 70 is associated with increased risk for other family members, and in such families the sex distribution is near equal. Alzheimer's disease occurs far more often than the other dementias. It comes on insidiously, without prodromal depression or anxiety, the first indication being failing short-term memory. This may be accompanied by a paranoid stage, because the patient blames other people for things he cannot find or has forgotten to buy. Emotions become blunted and sphincter control impaired: apathy supervenes.

Multi-infarct or arteriosclerotic dementia occurs slightly more commonly in men, usually in their late 60s and 70s. Blood pressure is high and the dementia typically comes on abruptly after a minor stroke. The symptoms are patchy, with the personality often unaffected, and the course progressive in steps. The man is frequently depressed.

Pick's disease, only having a 5 per cent frequency of occurrence compared to Alzheimer's, usually comes on as early as 40 but peaks at 60; it affects twice as many women as men. Most cases arise sporadically, but as in Alzheimer's disease, in some families there is a distinct genetic link. Notable features are a fatuous euphoria and overactivity alternating with apathy. Deterioration is steady.

Creutzfeldt-Jakob disease is a galloping dementia causing hallucinations, delusions and widespread neurological symptoms, with death within two years. It affects men and women equally, at ages 40 to 60. It is produced by a slow virus, related to that causing encephalopathy in cows.

Huntington's chorea: this terrible disease is strongly hereditary through a single autosomal dominant gene. Although it can appear at any age it strikes most often between 25 and 50, when the victim may already be married and have children. They stand a 50 per cent chance of developing the disease. The incidence is equal for the sexes but the symptoms of violence, outwardly directed or suicidal, and active sexual disturbances, cause more distress when the patient is a man, and are likely to bring him into conflict with the law. Involuntary movements deteriorate into profound muscular weakness and dementia supervenes.

Korsakoff's psychosis is usually a sequel to Wernicke's encephalopathy but may follow carbon monoxide poisoning, encephalitis lethargica or other causes of damage to specific memory circuits. It is commoner in men, probably because of the usual alcohol-related origin, and crops up between 45 and 55, at the peak of a man's career. It is characterized by disruption of the sense of time and gross difficulty in learning and registering anything new – even such emotionally-charged events as the death of a wife. Associated with these features is a propensity to confabulate – filling in from previous experience gaps in short-term memory. A bed-bound man may describe a country walk he took 'yesterday'. Intellectual powers, established knowledge, conversational and social skills are almost unaffected so the profound incapacity may not be picked up, at, say, a board meeting or a prestigious social event. Treatment seldom helps.

Alcoholic dementia occurs more often in women and at a later age than Korsakoff's disorder. There is global cognitive failure, resembling Alzheimer's disease but, unlike the latter, it is reversible in some cases. If alcohol is completely forsworn for several years, the brain becomes less shrunken and the intellectual powers revive (Lishman 1987).

HIV dementia: because of specific homosexual anal activity, more frequent casual sex of any type, especially abroad, and drug abuse with needle-sharing in prisons and elsewhere, men are far more at risk of HIV infection in the west than women. The nervous system is frequently involved very early. Apart from opportunistic infections such as cytomegalovirus encephalitis, and brain tumour, the brain cells may be directly invaded by the HI virus. The result is a startling fall off in intellectual function in a young man who as yet may seem perfectly healthy. Progress is inexorable.

Head injury happens much more frequently to the male. It may have chronic sequelae such as epilepsy in 5 per cent, and the 'frontal lobe syndrome' of lack of judgement, euphoria, lack of control of aggression, and outbursts of emotion punctuating general sluggishness. The repeated buffeting of the brain in boxers can lead to a chronic encephalopathy, with memory problems, difficulty in articulating and in balance, merging into dementia.

Chapter ten

Personality problems

Everyone has a personality: an established pattern of behaviour, ways of reacting and attitudes. A well-known example is the man with a short fuse who blows up into shouting or worse at the slightest provocation and keeps his family and colleagues on tenterhooks. Personality arises from constitution, from example and training at home, school and the outside world, and from individual circumstances. These include health and wealth, position in family and life-events, particularly the adverse ones. Potent influences are early separation, bereavement, physical or sexual abuse, accident or major illness, real poverty, a single parent, and so on. Age also has a marked effect on personality, although traits of immaturity may extend through the life-span in lack of responsibility and foresight, difficulties in self-discipline, dependency and inability to stand frustration; altruism is out. At the other pole, advancing age leads more or less rapidly to rigidity of views, hatred and fear of change, intolerance, loss of humour, increasing caution and a shrinking of interests except self-concern.

There are also male and female stereotypes which have validity. They are influenced by the sex steroids and powerfully by parental expectations. Traditional masculine traits include dominance, decisiveness, sexual energy, courage and resourcefulness, and a sense of power which may manifest either in bullying or protectiveness to the weak. Masculine drive may result in great achievements, literally reaching the moon or splitting the atom, or in damaging aggression. Homosexual men often combine artistic talent and sensitivity with male aggressivity, expressed in paranoid touchiness.

Personality disorders

These comprise characteristics which are exaggerated to a degree that causes discomfort or distress to the individual and disturbs the reasonable harmony of his relationships. Each category of personality disorder is coloured by sex. In general, because they are more given to action than women, men with personality disorders are liable to wreak the greatest havoc.

One type of personality disorder is seldom recognized or so labelled in men – the hysterical or histrionic personality. Yet such features as vanity, exhibitionism, and denial, shown in lying and pretence, are certainly seen in males. They usually crop up in the severe type of personality disorder associated with young, delinquent men – the socio-paths. Society suffers through these conscienceless, reckless men, but they too suffer. Over 70 per cent have a major depression, unbearable tension, and abysmally low self-opinion based on gross deprivation either physically or in affection during childhood. Their intelligence and the ability to make a good first impression are unimpaired, which opens up the feasibility of confidence tricks and sexual and other crimes. The inhibitions of moral values and the fear of punishment are meaningless to the sociopath. These men are characteristically strongly extrovert: blame is directed outwards, and intolerable boredom and tension take over rapidly during any work-like activity, so no job lasts. Always there is a hunger for stimulus – loud music or motor bikes, loud colours, drugs, varied sex and company. Alcohol and minor tranquillizers such as Valium increase extroversion and are particularly dangerous for a sociopath, making him more accident prone and more likely to commit an offence.

The sociopath is at the extreme of personality disorder and overlaps with both neuroses and psychoses, running into one or the other sporadically. Pinel, in 1801, described 'manie sans délire' to explain a condition, short of madness, which was as disrupting then as now. Women can have serious personality problems but do not have the drive to become out-and-out aggressive sociopaths. Even Myra Hindley, who is not far off, would not have committed a run of sadistic child murders had it not been for her involvement with her lover, Brady. Prisons and psychiatric hospitals house a high proportion of sociopaths. Treatment or management is difficult and usually disappointing, even at specialist centres such as Grendon Psychiatric Prison, which is geared to deal with dangerous offenders of this personality, or the Henderson Hospital. The latter employs the therapeutic community approach for the grossly personality-disordered of both sexes, whose lives are devastated by their persistently maladaptive outlook and actions.

Rather than applying the label sociopath and offering a standard regimen, the man's whole problem system requires evaluation. Then parts of it, at least, may be dealt with. Medical and psychiatric problems, for instance, asthma or an anxiety state, demand thorough treatment. Social issues – difficulties at work, with money, or housing – may need attention; while relationships may be a strength to build upon if there is someone who still cares, or – more often – a source of ongoing resentment. Attitudes are crucial: to sex and money, drugs and alcohol, any interests, self-opinion shown in paranoid reactions or self-mutilation. Problems with the law and attitude to the police may be recurrent problems. Group and individual opportunities to talk about himself, share his feelings and find himself accepted, and the chance to ventilate anger verbally, support the sociopath over time. There is also a need for facilities and help with vigorous competitive sport. For a fit, restless, tense young man, brimming with energy, passively to watch a football match is asking the unnatural. The man's response to treatment must be expected to include lying, unreliability, frequent non-compliance and complete ingratitude, with no glimmer of change for months, maybe years. It is not hopeless. Prevention begins too far back for today's youngsters. There needs to be immensely greater help and support for young, feckless parents, with easy access to nurseries and holidays.

One other kind of personality problem is also more or less confined to men – the Type A personality. This includes chronic tension, competitiveness and aggressive drive as in sociopathy but, instead of instant personal gratification, it is directed towards work-related achievements. The A-man's lack of care for others – except in the context of serving his ambitions – is also similar to the sociopathic state. Both types tend to overuse alcohol without being dependent on it. Ruthless selfishness is the hallmark of both, but the result in each differs drastically. The Type A man has the foresight to avoid legal or financial trouble for himself, but neither type counts the personal cost of his actions. His own health and peace of mind, and the effects on his relationships are treated as irrelevant. The sociopath provides little but excitement and short-lived spending sprees for those associated with him, but the Type A man ensures for himself – and whoever is with him

– expensive houses, cars, clothes and travel. Wives often stay for these perks. Sociopaths land in external trouble, mainly the law. Type A men have internal trouble – in the coronary circulation and the duodenum. Helping a Type A man depends on convincing him that his work activities will be curtailed willy-nilly if he does not modify his life-style. Only a minor adjustment can be anticipated.

The remaining categories of personality disorder are common to both sexes, but masculine gender influences their effects. An obsessionally houseproud woman is irritating to live with, but an obsessional man may become a sadistic schoolmaster or try to run his family Victorian-style and with grinding meanness. He is never pleased and seldom satisfied. A cyclothyme with changing moods may be an emotional woman. A man of the same nature may be an inconsistent colleague and an unpredictable boss. At home he is either low, and draining everyone's reserves that way, or full of ideas and energy, wearing them out with his restless activity. There is little to choose between paranoid people of either sex, but men may be definitely frightening. Women more often develop a paranoid outlook as they become older, but the withdrawn, schizoid personality is more often seen in males – at any age from puberty.

All personality disorders are modified by the person's sex – with more expressivity and histrionics in women, and more aggression in men. An inadequate dependent woman clings and cries and spoils her partner's life in this way, while the same type of personality in a man is likely to result in passive aggression: undermining his companions' comfort with quiet resentments, blocking rather than confronting.

Chapter eleven

Alcohol and drug abuse

Man's basic needs are food, clothing and shelter. To make life bearable he also needs love and some release from what Rouché terms 'the intolerable clutch of reality' – the never-ending treadmill of living. Substances that magically relax the tyranny of mind and memory have been used as far back as history records. For thousands of years alcohol has been made from the fermentation of almost any carbohydrate-containing material. References in the Old Testament mention Noah getting drunk and the use of wine as a libation in the Temple. In New Testament times it was the accepted festive drink: witness the water-into-wine miracle at the wedding feast. Particularly in Europe and North America alcohol is established as the predominant social drug, kept in every home and wherever men – specifically – meet. Drinking alcohol is almost universally regarded as standard masculine practice – which women may also enjoy.

Before knowledge and expertise in chemistry evolved during the early nineteenth century, the only other mind- and mood-altering substances came from plants. These may require special climatic conditions. Hemp – cannabis – was used medically and for mood as far back as 2700 BC in China and continues to be used extensively in the Far and Middle East, ousting alcohol in the Muslim world. When alcoholism from childhood to the grave was endemic among the poor, and interfered with profit in nineteenth century industrial Britain, taxation was introduced to curb the use of drink – successfully. Those many seeking solace turned to opium and its derivatives – the so-called 'flowers of happiness'. They were readily available over the grocer's counter. Cocaine – recommended by Sigmund Freud as good medicine – was used to combat fatigue and depression. 'Magic' mushrooms were used in South America for their interesting effects on perception (Vaillant 1983).

Synthetic preparations have become increasingly available over the last 150 years. The first such psychotropic was chloral hydrate. Heroin came out in 1898 and methadone in the Second World War. Designer drugs, like crack and Ecstasy, are recent additions to the repertoire. The illegal drug trade has grown so rich and well organized that great countries like the US and the USSR are losing through drug abuse an unacceptably large number of those in what should be their most productive years. Colombia – in 1989 – was almost in a state of civil war over the problem. As with alcohol, it is men who are most likely to be drug casualties. Soldiers in danger, discomfort and boredom abroad try anything that promises some change. Travellers and explorers also bring home plants and herbs to smoke or chew. They are mainly men, and even in the mean streets of Soho, it is men who are the more adventurous or reckless, both as traders and users.

Despite the devastation caused by other drugs, including the enhanced spread of HIV infection from shared needles for injectables, alcohol still affects the lives of many more people. The consumption of alcohol and also its abuse are increasing in the USA and UK – especially among women in the latter. Men have a big headstart, however. Death from alcohol-related disease now occurs most often in the early 50s, compared with 60, ten years ago. France leads the world in deaths from cirrhosis. Other serious physical damage from alcohol includes pancreatitis, cardiomyopathy, cancers of the mouth, larynx, oesophagus and liver, peptic ulcer, peripheral neuropathy, toxic psychoses and dementia. Indirect but potentially lethal harm comes from overdosage – 64 per cent are associated with alcohol – and completed suicide, assault and accidents. In Glasgow one-third of acute male surgical admissions are for head injury and more than 50 per cent of these are due to alcohol (Solomon and Keeley 1982).

Risk factors

Genetic influences have been demonstrated by twin and adoption studies (Chapter 4). There is also a racial effect. Koreans, Chinese and Japanese are less able to clear their systems of acetaldehyde: they look more flushed and are more liable to circulatory upset than Caucasians, when they drink. Eskimos and certain American Indian groups are particularly slow to sober up after an alcoholic bout. Apart from male sex and genetics there are numerous other important vulnerability factors for alcohol excess.

Cultural and social expectations are key. In France there is no stigma in drinking – lightly or heavily – whereas in Utah or Saudi it is strongly disapproved. Irishmen are expected to drink generously unless they have taken the pledge, but Jewish men with control. Social class is relevant only in that while professional men often damage their mental or physical health through alcohol, it is not acceptable for them deliberately to have a piss up and get fighting drunk like football fans. In 5 BC the Greeks had to ban the bringing of alcohol into their stadiums on pain of a fine, much as occurs at football matches now.

The concept of an addictive personality is often considered, but the sociopathy and depression sometimes seen in heavy drinkers provides a chicken and egg dilemma. It does seem that alcohol is used largely to alleviate tension, so the chronically tense individual is at risk. Other predisposing factors are definite psychiatric disorders, such as schizophrenia, manic depression, depression and severe personality problems. Poverty, all forms of deprivation, and particularly 'having seen better days', make fertile soil for the development of alcoholic excess. Precipitating factors include psychological crises with acute anxiety or depression and insomnia, or social crises such as separation, bereavement, job loss or isolation.

The alcohol habit develops insidiously. Its rewarding effect – relaxation – is immediate. The adverse effects of shorter life and less money are long delayed. Learning is geared to obvious and rapid results. This is why slimming is so difficult – the reward for self-control is so slow. The environment and company, usually warm and congenial, associated with drinking sets off the 'thirst', for instance, friends, the pub crowd, a golf club, a get-together with colleagues.

Habit once established makes drinking an automatic, unconsidered response. Fatigue, frustration, boredom, pain, worry, irritation, depression – all are interpreted as the 'need' for a drink. Introverts may well benefit psychologically from a modicum of alcohol to loosen their rigidity. They are less often drinkers than the extroverts who definitely do not need alcohol. It may push them into impulsivity, recklessness and untrammelled gratification of the whim of the moment.

The alcohol syndrome

This develops along predictable lines. At first there is increased tolerance, and the heavy drinker boasts that he 'can take it' and does not get drunk. This stage is due to stimulation of the microsomal liver enzymes so that they can cope with large quantities of alcohol and incidentally of other drugs. Next comes the phase of repeated mild withdrawal effects: low mood in the mornings, with nausea; tremor; night sweats. Lowered blood sugar may confuse the picture, so that the man may appear to be more drunk than he is and the glucose he needs for his hypoglycaemia not given. During alcoholism in full flower the man broadens his choice of drinks to include everything alcoholic. As the disorder progresses the repertoire narrows until only one type of drink is used. The major physical and mental complications are now obvious. Weight, which may have increased earlier on, as in 'beer belly', drains away. As liver failure sets in the man's tolerance to alcohol diminishes, to his puzzlement and distress (Edwards and Grant 1977).

The results of alcohol excess

These are manifest and direct, affecting the man's brain and body, or secondary:

Stress in the family

An alcoholic man in the house brings social isolation on the family, through their shame and embarrassment. Financial hardship, lying, quarrels, infidelity and violence invade the home. The man may not be able to do his work, or not be allowed, for instance, to drive. His parents, or more often, his wife and children, may have to take on his responsibilities, but there is a resentful, non-cohesive atmosphere – unlike the 'pulling together' of a normal family during hard times.

Nearly 70 per cent of the wives of alcoholics are clinically anxious, but they become less disturbed as the situation becomes chronic. Some women appear to need a weak and incompetent man, but cope excellently when he is *hors de combat*. Often the wife has a roller-coaster ride, with her husband alternating between being a child or a tyrant.

The children of alcoholics frequently underachieve at school and run a greater risk of truancy and conduct disorders. More seriously, children of alcoholic fathers or stepfathers are much likelier than the norm to suffer neglect or actual abuse, physical or sexual.

Work

Even a small quantity of alcohol in the blood, well below the legal driving limit, impairs a man's motor, sensory and psychomotor function. His judgement is untrustworthy and accidents are common. He is difficult to work with because of his cantankerousness and unpredictability. He is often late or absent for work, especially on Mondays. By preretirement, on average, the chronic alcoholic works only 25 per cent of the time he should.

Sexual activity

This is increased in the expansive early stages, with little regard for the woman's feelings. The longer term effects are universally detrimental. Libido is reduced and various forms of dysfunction occur. The man is prone to try different partners and perversions in an attempt to overcome his difficulties, and morbid jealousy, either homosexual or heterosexual, easily develops.

Crime

The combination of shortage of money – drained away on drink or drugs – and inefficient management leads to debt, stealing and not 'wasting' money on food or clothes for self or family. Violent crime including homicide is commonly associated with the Dutch courage of alcohol. Forty per cent of male prisoners in Britain habitually use alcohol excessively and turn to it immediately they are discharged, making resettlement difficult. One-third of men on remand or in prison after conviction are addicted to heroin or cocaine according to a Social Services survey in 1989.

Traffic and other accidents

These are much more frequent in drinkers. Suicide is also far commoner in these patients. Alcohol is, after all, a depressant.

The psychiatric sequelae of excess drinking are dealt with in other parts of the book. Suffice it to say that while men in particular see alcohol as a panacea for depressive and anxiety symptoms, while there may be evanescent relief, the effect of continued use is detrimental in both states.

Organic syndromes are usually progressive and in the mild, early stages far more frequent than is generally recognized. Who does not know a highly-placed executive who has not had a new idea since he was 50, and worse, cannot grasp a fresh concept from anyone else? The ability to grind out the old platitudes is undimmed.

Treatment

For either alcoholism or drug addiction, treatment is long, tortuous and disappointing. The famous Rand Report of 1976 showed a 53 per cent remission rate in alcoholism for those who had only one contact with an agency, compared with an overall rate of 68 per cent, and 73 per cent if all the stops were pulled out for two years plus, in favourable cases. Women may sometimes be moved by personal appeals and sentiment to alter their bad habits. Men never give up alcohol or other drugs for wives, mothers, lovers or children. They do respond to suspension from work, however. It is disgraceful that in Britain, unlike other western countries, so few big companies or government departments provide a facility for dealing with these common problems. The proposition to put a health warning on bottles and cans of alcoholic drinks, as on cigarette packets, is a forlorn hope (Edwards and Grant 1980).

Chapter twelve

Sexual problems

Interest in sex and the physiological responses to it are far livelier in the male. He is almost always the initiator of intercourse and necessarily more vigorous in carrying it out. It follows that men – with their powerful drive – are more likely to get caught up in various deviations, run into difficulties with the law, or develop sexually-transmitted diseases, including HIV infection.

Dysfunction

Only this group of sexual problems affects men and women approximately equally, the latter mainly through psychological inhibition. The first step towards intercourse is desire, more compelling in the male. It proceeds with arousal accompanied by erection, a stage of increasing excitement, then orgasm demonstrated by emission and ejaculation. Resolution is the final phase of physical and emotional relief and relaxation.

Low libido may be primary – the man has never been interested or even curious, and frankly is not worried; or it may be secondary, and he is very concerned. Serious illness, diabetes, chronic brain syndromes, alcohol in any but minimal dosage, and various drugs: major tranquillizers, barbiturates and spironolactone, may all reduce libido (Beeley 1982). Oestrogen and the anti-androgen cyproterone acetate are used to diminish libido in some cases of repeated sex crime. Increased libido may result from irritation of the neck of the bladder, as in prostatic enlargement – the usual reason when an elderly bishop behaves with importunity in public – or with small amounts of alcohol, or the notorious Spanish fly. Aphrodisiacs in general do not have a physiological effect but act through suggestion. Charles II used cocoa with good effect. In some deviations desire is compulsive.

There is a curious sharp reduction of desire in 'spectatoring'. The man's libido switches off as soon as he starts the act. He completes it mechanically taking a detached interest in the process, either because he is extremely narcissistic or he would prefer a different partner.

Dysfunction in the performance consists of erectile impotence in 53 per cent, premature ejaculation in 15 per cent and in 7 per cent absent or delayed ejaculation. Organic factors are often a factor in these difficulties, particularly diabetes and drugs. Erection may be impaired by hypotensives, major tranquillizers, tricyclic antidepressants, disulfiram, digoxin, clofibrate and antihistamines. Ejaculation is put out by thioridazine and the monoamine-oxidase inhibitors (MAOIs). In all cases sexual anxiety is important. The fear of failure, so deeply felt by the male in this area, comes from inexperience, being out of practice for whatever reason, an excessively demanding woman perhaps trying for a pregnancy, or the man's own extreme wish to please his partner. Criticism, sarcasm, the memory of failure on previous occasions, or, dating from childhood, the lack of a trustworthy, committed relationship from parents or others makes the dread of rejection paralysing. Treatment starts with discussion of attitudes with the man and his partner, then runs through sensate focusing and graded stimulation, until in 80 per cent of cases the problem resolves. For those with intractable organically-based erectile problems, self-injection of the penis on each occasion, or surgical insertion of an inflatable or rigid prosthesis may be used.

Ejaculatory difficulties are treated by superstimulation – again the partner must help. Low libido may be improved by selected pornographic films and pictures, and psychotherapy. Anxiety-reducing manoeuvres are useful in all cases and, of course, organic problems must be recognized and if possible dealt with (Cole 1985).

Sexual deviations

These amount to a group of sexual behaviours seen as abnormal, harmful or morally wrong according to western culture and current fashion. Especially since about 1960, attitudes have become increasingly tolerant, notably in regard to homosexuality, oral and – tacitly – anal intercourse. Deviations presently recognized comprise disorders of orientation and of gender role. The former include paedophilia, rape, exhibitionism, frotteurism, voyeurism ('Peeping Toms'), fetishism, sado-masochism, and some rare oddities. Gender role anomalies are transvestism and transsexualism. All of these disorders are almost entirely male problems.

Homosexuality

Homosexuality, or orientation towards the same sex, is in a special class. It affects men and women, but lesbianism is less obvious and poses no physical or health threat to anyone.

Predominantly homosexual men, a minority of about 10 per cent, claim passionately that their preference is a variant, if not an improvement, on normal. From Ancient Greece to Kinsey adult males have commonly enjoyed some sexual contact with other men. It is endemic in submarines, monasteries, prisons, or wherever men live in a one-sex community for prolonged periods. Exclusive homosexuality clearly cannot be viable in nature, but it has always been a feature of civilizations in decline. Because of legal restrictions on homosexual acts involving any male under 21, the umbrella crime of gross indecency and mistrust of the integrity of homosexuals, many still hide their orientation. Discovery of homosexual practices has led to public disgrace or prophylactic resignation among politicians, even in the last decade, but actors increasingly often come out of the closet waving a banner.

Although there is some evidence of a genetic link in some and of low levels of testosterone in others, two other causative factors are even more frequent: family patterning, and, in some youngsters of a critical age in stark financial straits, expedience. The common family set-up comprises a detached or rigid and hostile father – from a headmaster to an alcoholic – and a mother who naturally indulges in emotionality and intimacy in her relationships. Without any such intention, she often uses her son to compensate for a lack of understanding and affection in the marriage. The homosexual son is often attractive and the youngest, protected by his mother from his father, big brothers or school bullies. A frequent result is the development of immanent insecurity with excessive fear of physical injury. Artistic sensitivity and expressivity are characteristic of homosexual men, as are creative culinary skills that surpass those of women. While they enjoy the company of women, particularly older women, the charming manners of gays are sprinkled through with snide anti-female digs. They are revolted at the thought of physical intimacy with a woman, even of brushing against her breasts in a lift.

Obsession with the penis – their own and others – is universal and forms a large part of the attraction of multiple contacts or just watching in public lavatories and on commons. Homosexuals may flaunt their gay condition or dress and behave with rigid formality. Similarly their choice of partner is either a model of masculinity or a pretty, girlish boy. The homosexual loves to be reminded of and identify with his own youth. His essential insecurity tends to make him touchy, putting a strain on relationships. The same insecurity leads to compulsive urges for the reassurance of sexual contact, regardless of risks. The parents react in a predictable way. At first both are horrified and ashamed, if both know, but often only the mother is in her son's confidence – and is 'understanding'. This excludes the father. Fathers are liable to be angry and intolerant – like the mothers of lesbian daughters – presumably because of the threat to their own sexuality.

The impact of AIDS on the homosexual community – after a mini-rehearsal in the early 1980s with Herpes genitalis – has led to a great deal of constructive co-operation, modification of sexual practices, and an admirable degree of courage: AIDS is discussed at the end of this chapter.

Most homosexual men today have seen friends fade and die, with HIV infection. Aside from this the main impediment to a happy life as a homosexual is the inevitability of ageing, in a community which rejects the older man – 35 plus – unless he is wealthy. Alcoholism and suicide both hold enhanced risk for homosexuals (West 1983).

Paedophilia

This has always been a minority interest. In 1985 it achieved notoriety in Britain with a huge cluster of cases of child sexual abuse in Cleveland. These were uncovered and exaggerated by over-enthusiastic diagnosis, but were nevertheless a worrying number. Although homosexuals are often considered the major danger to children, in fact more than 70 per cent of child victims are female. Some are mere infants, but the likeliest age for abused girls is 7 to 9 years, while boys are usually 11 plus, merging into adolescence. Most paedophiles are timid men with low self-esteem, sometimes with a mild handicap. They find it easier to approach children and either bribe or dominate them. The long-term effects on the children may be disruption of the normal development of sexuality, especially if a trusted relative or family friend is the man in question: this is the usual scenario.

Mothers and other women may be seductive to little boys, but very rarely force sexual interference on children; paedophiles are mainly male. Whichever their orientation, they are attracted into work as schoolteachers, scoutmasters, and workers in children's homes or with adolescents. Men in these professions, whether paedophile or homosexual, are well advised to seek therapy. This consists of behavioural and other psychotherapy, tranquillizers or other anti-androgenic medication. It is moderately effective if the man accepts and persists with it; many only do so while under legal compulsion.

Rape

The victim is almost always a female of any age from infant to geriatric, but most frequently aged 15 to 20. It commonly arises in those who have committed other crimes. Some men need the excitement of – say – a burglary, to become sexually aroused. The essence of rape is the domination and humiliation of the female. Sometimes the trigger is rejection including within a marriage. The American method of group therapy, in which rapists and victims confront one another and discuss their feelings, is more constructive than punishment alone. The only benefit of imprisonment itself is the immediate satisfaction of the girl and her family. Re-offending is appallingly common. As with paedophilia, rapists are known to their victims more often than not.

Exhibitionism

By contrast, this male deviation is a nuisance rather than a menace. The usual targets are schoolgirls, and the aim is to shock and impress them by a primitive display of masculinity. Exhibitionism does not lead into rape, but it is wise for the girl not to laugh or jeer at the man. Occasionally such men hit out if humiliated.

Frotteurism

Rubbing the genitals, usually against a woman's bottom in a crowded place like a tube train, is also more nuisance than danger. Women do nothing similar.

Voyeurism ('Peeping Toms')

Voyeurs who haunt the bushes in public parks also pose little physical danger to others. Pornographic films and videos cater for this perversion. It involves a few female viewers.

Fetishism

A limited element of this quirk lies within the bounds of normality. Spike heels, frilly black panties and can-can dancers' garters are examples. Rubber gear is oddly popular. Fetishism, a sexual response to an inanimate object, becoming necessary for intercourse to take place, can be produced experimentally, and can equally be extinguished by reward/aversion therapy.

Sado-masochism

A degree of receiving and inflicting pain in play is a normal part of sexual intercourse: 'I could eat you up', 'I could hug you to death', and the commonplace 'love-bites' illustrate this. The popularity in England of the game of spanking and being spanked and insulted is well known and within the repertoire of most prostitutes. Bondage is also frequently practised, to or by the man, and sometimes accidentally causes physical harm. In general men are more sadistic, women more masochistic, but sadism and masochism are two facets of the same distorted self-image. The sado-masochist believes that no one would voluntarily accept him or her sexually, unless forced into it by cruelty of which sex is a part, or invited into it by the abject appeal for the lover to do whatever he will. Swinburne extolled 'Our Lady of Pain' and 'roses and raptures of vice' in his poem 'Dolores'. The compulsion to cause pain, powered by frustrated male sexual drive, can become so dangerous as to result in lust-murder. Series of such murders have caused dread and distress in whole communities until the man is caught. The murderer may seem of apparently normal mentality, but well-concealed schizophrenia may make a major contribution in some cases. Peter Sutcliffe turned out to be one such. The behaviour of these men is both extreme and bizarre. Compulsive masochism may manifest in the course of a depressive illness (Christie Brown 1983).

Gender role deviations

Transvestism

Transvestism, cross-dressing, is only of real significance in men. The symptomatic type is either a form of fetishism or hephephilia (the man needs to be wearing female clothing for sexual excitement), or it is an adjunct to homosexuality. Simple transvestism, present in 1 in 30,000 men in the UK, is not motivated by sexual gratification. It relieves anxiety, providing the cross-dresser with an escape from his lack of a sense of security and self-esteem. Transvestites are often married and have moderately happy relationships with their wives, with sex something of minor importance. Ruth Rendell's short story, *The New Girl Friend*, illustrates the pleasure a co-operative woman can give a transvestite by playing out his game with him. Many wives are horrified and the man's propensity is a secret. Treatment is usually neither sought nor effective.

Transsexualism

In this condition, four times as common in males as females at 1 in 34,000, the man is convinced that he is really a woman, cruelly trapped in an inappropriate body. The wish to change physically into a woman is so powerful that the man will travel anywhere and pay anything for surgery. He begs for female hormone medication. Psychotherapy aimed at altering the man's convictions is useless, but he will need psycho-therapeutic support in any event. The general rule is to consider plastic surgery only if the man has managed to live successfully as a woman for two years. Sometimes, in the early stages of schizophrenia, a man may feel that he is changing sex – or that his head or body are altering in shape – but most transsexuals are neurotic, not psychotic.

Sexual crimes

These are almost entirely confined to men, partly because there are fewer ways in which women can break the law. The strong, sometimes compulsive, sexual urge in men can override good sense and inhibitions, especially if drink or drugs that relax are involved, or the man is aroused by an exciting situation. Historically, soldiers fresh from battle have indulged in pillage – and rape. Crime, including violent crime, includes a similar element of danger.

Other sexual crimes are buggery, sexual intercourse with boys under 15 and adolescent males under 21 – by a man, or with girls under 16. There are various grades of assault and gross indecency which cover a range of offensive behaviours. These include some not unwelcomed masturbatory activity between men in public places.

The commonest offence is exhibitionism. Usually one court appearance is sufficient warning, but the act is more likely to be repetitive and ominous if the victim is a prepubertal girl. This implies a paedophilic interest, which may develop. Paedophilic rapists and men for whom sexual activity is part of personal aggression are likely to repeat their assaultive behaviour, becoming increasingly dangerous. Friends and relatives of such men are often afraid to voice their suspicions to the police. Another group which may fail to come forward are the wives or common law wives of fathers or stepfathers who commit incest. There is tacit condonation (Chiswick 1983).

Sexually-transmitted diseases (STD)

Men have long outnumbered women by about 2 to 1 in problems with STD, but from the early 1960s until the advent of HIV infection, the ratio was becoming more equal. Before the early 1980s the most troublesome psychological difficulty in STD was venereophobia, an irrational conviction of having contracted a disorder, or complaint about symptoms long after they had been cured. This was in contrast to the robust attitude of most men contracting a disease through sexual activity. Venereophobia escalated in 1983–4 when there was an increase in Herpes genitalis. Publicity made everyone aware of its basic incurability and the dire effects on women and their babies, but 'herpes angst' was swept aside by the far greater dangers of AIDS.

HIV infection

In the west but not the Third World the immuno-deficiency virus has affected primarily homosexual males, with an increasing number of intravenous drug users. The latter can be of either sex, but more men are involved. Many in the homosexual and bisexual communities have modified their life- and sex-styles, leading to a slowdown of the rate of increase in HIV cases. Nevertheless, in a survey in Britain in 1988, it was found that 60 per cent had engaged in passive and 62 per cent in active anal intercourse in the past twelve months. Twenty-five per cent felt the use of a condom was unacceptable; the number of partners ranged from 0 to 200. The drug users are less amenable to changing their habits, although the fashion among some for snorting heroin is to be welcomed. The male prison population presents a problem. There is a high prevalence of drug abuse – up to 50 per cent of the inmates – with a dearth of clean needles and syringes. An added risk is the sexual activity between the men, whether or not heterosexual outside.

Anxiety and depression are common, understandable reactions to a diagnosis of HIV infection, or to some of the vague symptoms considered characteristic. The development of Kaposi's sarcoma or other clear indications of AIDS may lead others to shun the victim so that he is left alone with his disease. Not all doctors are emotionally geared to cope with such cases, but support is available through special clinics, voluntary organizations such as the Terrence Higgins Trust and telephone agencies. More serious than the neurotic sufferings are the organic effects, either by direct viral invasion of the brain or through opportunistic infections – unopposed by the body's defences – of brain or meninges. A subacute, and occasionally an acute, organic brain syndrome results. Direct infiltration of the neurones by the AIDS virus often occurs before other symptoms of AIDS appear. The patient, at an inappropriately young age, develops all the manifestations of dementia, progressing as in Alzheimer's disease. One ray of hope: AIDS dementia complex shows a declining incidence in patients treated with zidovudine. This recently developed drug appears to inhibit replication of HIV in the central nervous system (Portegies *et al.* 1989).

Chapter thirteen

Work, family and psychosomatics

Throughout history men have identified with their work: bricklayer, vicar, accountant. To lose their job, whether by ill health, retirement or redundancy, is to lose themselves and their sense of personal value. Until very recently women, by contrast, were assessed for status and social class on their fathers' and then their husbands' occupations. By nature and by training men are markedly competitive. The added group of females jockeying for the best or the scarce posts pose an extra threat to the security and accustomed position of men. Although women are coming out of the closet into medicine, cab-driving, stockbroking, their success is still not measured just on material values and prestige. Family and emotional parameters rate in a way that they never do for men.

Work for a man provides a feeling of achievement, pride in his expertise, and an assured place in society and at home. It gives him a sense of belonging among colleagues and the opportunity for satisfying relationships. His day, week, life runs in a rhythm of alternating work and leisure. Importantly it provides money: for survival, shelter, family and the pleasures of holidays and hobbies. Payment provides regular proof of being needed.

The greatest work-related stress for a man, but not for a woman, is losing his job. Even the threat of job-loss is associated with a 60 per cent increase in visits to the family doctor, and a raised incidence of parasuicide. Unemployment itself goes with double the usual mortality in men, from a wide range of illness. There is a greater likelihood of both suicide and parasuicide (Platt 1986). Smoking and drinking also increase during periods without work, undermining physical and psychological health (Bolton and Oatley 1987). The likelihood of re-employment is reduced. Lack of a proper job is a problem for men: women, with their different values for personal worth are less upset, and are also better able to give or to receive emotional support. Women make meals for their friends in distress and spend time talking with them: men buy each other a drink.

The effect of losing his job is like a bereavement to a man, and similarly it goes through predictable phases. The first is one of shock and disbelief, especially if the change was sudden. The second is an unrealistically optimistic stage. The man sees the loss as temporary, and anyway a welcome chance to relax and catch up with jobs around the home. After about three weeks this honeymoon phase fades, and he misses the security of a structured life, somewhere to go, and earning. Money may be limited. Every day is passed in meaningless leisure. Inertia creeps on, with waning of energy, interest and self-esteem. Attempts to find work are unexpectedly, then routinely, unavailing. Irritability develops and so do family tensions. Nearly 20 per cent of the wives of unemployed men suffer from anxiety or depression compared with 1.3 per cent of those whose husbands are in work (Penkower et al. 1988). Feelings of inferiority and helplessness lead into deep unhappiness or a clinical depression – in men out of work. Especially vulnerable are the young and the old, immigrants and the unskilled – even after planned retirement. An extrovert, optimistic personality ameliorates the adverse effects. Other types are liable to become chronically embittered, hopeless and anxious.

Psychosomatic illness is common. Hypertension and associated cardiovascular disorders, duodenal ulcer and general digestive troubles, back pain, and asthma are particularly frequent in men, but stressed males are not immune from irritable colon, colitis, rheumatoid arthritis and migraine. Cancers are prone to develop or progress more rapidly when the immune mechanisms lose efficiency in long-term low mood and low self-esteem. Alcohol and tobacco may compound the issue. It is significant that while men who are working to strain levels are well known to develop coronary disease, cardiovascular disorders and death are likelier in recently retired or otherwise unemployed men of 45 plus, as with those who have suffered a major personal bereavement in the past twelve months.

For a man without work essential management comprises finding a need for his help outside the home. Domesticating a man at this stage, particularly if his wife is working, may seem sensible and convenient. In fact it is harmful and humiliating to make him a *hausfrau*. Better by far for his physical and mental well-being for him to wear himself out by continuing effort, whether or not with payment. Contact with people outside the family is necessary nourishment. REACH in London acts as a clearing house for executives prepared to give their skills for free.

While worst of all is to have none, work itself may be a stress – through the man's attitude to it. Since the early 1970s, when two dynamic American psychiatrists, Friedman and Rosenman, floated the concept, men have been considered to have Type *A* or Type *B* personalities. This applies mainly to their working practices. Although there are recent studies raising doubts about the mechanisms by which particular behaviours may do harm, it is generally accepted that highly competitive, intellectually aggressive and achievement-oriented men, always tense and impatient – Type *A* – commonly develop coronary heart disease (Rosenman 1974). Type *B* men, who pace themselves and are able to relax, are the survivors. However, to tell a Type *A* man that he must cut down his frenetic activity only enhances his stress, and the bodily reactions of raised cortisol and catecholamine production, fast pulse and increased blood pressure. Mental work induces these physiological responses in all personalities, but they are most marked in Type *A*. They put a strain on blood vessels and heart (Frankenhaeuser *et al.* 1980). Type *A* men, compared with Type *B*, are liable to be thrown by unforeseen life events. Although they take on extra work and responsibility eagerly, unexpected personal disaster – accident or illness hampering their activity, or loss by divorce or otherwise of a wife – can plunge them into feelings of frustration and impotence. Failure to respond effectively confirms the sense of helplessness. Everyone else is blamed, but this gives little relief. It is in this plight that heart attack is most likely (Weidner 1980).

Apart from the effect of a man's personality, the work itself may cause stress. In general it is not the top jobs that are most stressful, however huge the responsibility. What is most upsetting is a job in which high demands are made but the man has little control over policy, plans and the way he works. Work that is intellectually, and less often physically, beyond a man's capacity leads to depression mixed with anxiety, or to a psychosomatic disorder that allows him to go off sick. Too little to do and not enough responsibility cause frustration, irritability and finally lethargy. Type *A* men are particularly poor at tolerating inactivity. Personality clashes are likely, and especially in reaction to obsessional senior staff and uninterested juniors. Lack of supervision and feedback – apart from criticism – dismal training facilities and career prospects, repetitive routine, and unfair distribution of duties may make the job seem all drudgery and no satisfaction: with attendant stress-related problems.

It is a tragedy that only 35 per cent of men below retirement age return to work within 18 months of having a myocardial attack. It seems irrelevant whether or not they have residual symptoms. Forty per cent take early retirement, 16 per cent remain on everlasting convalescence and 10 per cent see themselves as out of work. Professional men and some upper management are usually working again within a few months – or weeks – but understandably only a quarter of heavy manual workers. A third of clerical, lower management and light manual workers get back to work. Far too little help is given to all these men, either by their employers or trade unions, to enable them to return to active, profitable life, even if not in precisely the same job. At the least, counselling services are needed because good, able men are being wasted and made to feel worthless (Watson *et al.* 1986).

Stress management programmes

Those offered at the workplace are most likely to be used – and useful. Twenty per cent of the larger corporations in California and Colorado provide general stress courses, and virtually all provide a problem-drinking service. Only a handful of companies do either in the UK, despite a very high incidence of heart disorders in particular (Rowe 1989). Many stress programmes are multimodal, and are aimed at the whole spectrum of stress at work, but with especial emphasis on side-stepping a second – preferably a first – heart attack. They comprise physical, educational and psychological elements. Information on a healthy diet and life-style, and the dangers to avoid including tobacco, social drugs and excessive alcohol, is provided. An aerobic exercise programme is instituted. Its object is to increase general fitness, with a reduction in blood pressure and in reactivity to mental challenges. The psychological component has several strands. Group discussions cover work, general policies and personal and interpersonal difficulties, and future aspirations. Such open communication helps to diffuse tensions.

A conceptual model of behaviour liable to lead to difficulties for the individual and others, and which may secondarily damage physical health is presented and examined. The participants are taught what cues to look for in physiology – for instance, muscle tension and pulse rate; behaviourally – for instance, hurry and impatience; and in thought – for instance, decisions without consideration of their effects on other people. These cues signal the start of a spiral of anxiety, frustration and irritability. This is the time to apply manoeuvres to damp down the level of arousal before it touches danger level. These may include meditation, relaxation techniques, autohypnosis, and arguing logically with oneself. What is essential is a break in current activity, preferably moving physically and talking on an unrelated subject with – anyone.

The only way a Type A man will buy the stress package is if he is convinced that he may be prevented from working otherwise. Even so some 30 per cent of these men are not highly reactive and some workers have found that neither exercise nor the whole stress management programme improves Type A men on physiological measures, relevant to the cardiac risks, although they claim to feel more relaxed and better at pacing themselves (Seraganian et al. 1987).

Burnout

Freudenburger coined the term in the early 1970s, with particular reference to health workers, the police and others working with the public. Managers – of people as well as business – were later included. The syndrome, described in men predominantly, comprises emotional exhaustion, physical fatigue, unrefreshing sleep, poor concentration, irritability and moodiness, proneness to accidents, and various bodily symptoms: headache, digestive discomfort, backache, and so on. Alcohol and tobacco use goes up; efficiency and harmony with colleagues declines. All this contains some elements of reactive depression, but it is more a matter of being fagged out by an unsatisfying job, a sense of receiving little support while being in the target zone for blame and criticism. Unsocial or excessively long hours are only a burden when they are for an employer: those with their own business seldom suffer burnout, no matter how long they work. Their marriages may suffer.

Burnout is a form of work stress disorder. The victim requires more interest to be shown in his efforts, with praise where it is due. The job should be analysed for stimulus and variety, and opportunities for advancement – then modified as necessary. As far as possible, in accordance with its size, the workplace should be pleasant and provide facilities for rest, relaxation and socializing, and easily available, cheap, soft drinks. Discussion groups are useful, providing a check on work practices and the chance of airing problems. A counsellor can discuss career, personal and health matters on an individual basis. Such arrangements and specific policies for alcohol-related problems are standard in North America, but only a few British firms run stress programmes (Mayou 1987).

Family matters

Although masculine values rate work ahead of people, this is not to say a man's relatives do not influence him. It is particularly difficult for a man with a brilliant father to fulfil his own potential. To compete with his father means certain defeat. Not to try brings certain failure. A mother who builds up her boy's confidence is a boon indeed, but one who smothers and protects leaves him handicapped in the real world of women, men and work. Controlling parents, who want to live – again – through their son prevent his free choice of a career or sexual partner. He may over-react and become a layabout, with friends to fit, or buckle under and remain permanently resentful and repressed. He is likely to marry out of his cultural group, whether Jewish, Jamaican or Muslim. This act of rebellion deprives the parents of the type of grandchildren for which they had planned.

Wives, whether common law or regular, probably have the deepest influence of all. A pretty, extravagant scatterbrain may be just the inspiration a man needs to make money. Children may have the same challenging effect, if expensive education is required. A working wife can be a splendid partner, but if she has too high a profile this can undermine the man's self-confidence – making him critical, petty and controlling. Motherly, dominant women also deflate a husband's self-image. Being looked after is so addictive that he may slip into dependency and a lack of responsibility. Wives who need weak partners are especially malignant in their effect on alcohol-prone men. Nevertheless – in spite of the snags – men live longer and are less liable to depression or anxiety if they are married. A stable, long-term homosexual relationship does not have this beneficial result. A good marriage helps a man through adverse life events such as job loss, and is best when intimacy and interests are shared. Unfortunately, in middle age, when a high-quality marital status is most needed, most marriages decay. Each partner is less satisfied with his or her life and less happy. In the marriage sex, mutual concerns and topics become scarce; almost anything is a reason for separate bedrooms, and the couple hold differing views on more subjects. While women are rehearsing for widowhood, at this stage men become increasingly obsessed with their health. They take to personal 'body-monitoring'. Nothing is as devastating to a man as a failure in his health, from 50 plus. In general men need lose little of the attributes of masculinity: vigour, strength, sexual performance and fertility. Competence and male courage continue.

However, to remain on form a middle-aged man must have the high regard of his family. Men whose wives are physically or psychiatrically ill become chronically anxious and depressed. If they are widowed they are at increased risk of serious illness or even death, mainly from heart trouble. Their children's opinion is also crucial:

Case: Josef, 59, was a highly-successful property developer in Israel. He came to England where his son was in a similar business. Because of his faulty English and lack of understanding of the market in Britain, he lost a lot of money. His humiliation before his son drove him to a desperate suicidal attempt by drowning.

The rivalry between father and son if they work together inevitably leads to frustration on the son's side, and by the father, ultimately a feeling of having been cruelly rejected, as he is encouraged to 'retire'. Women never suffer so acutely when work and family interact, but a mother who has been beautiful may suffer torments when her daughter outshines her.

Psychosomatics

Most illness can be seen at least in part as psychosomatic. The emotional state greatly affects the development and continuance of symptoms. Somatizers – those who tend to translate all their problems into physical disorders and then focus their anxiety on these – are more often women. Nevertheless, men are even less willing to accept that they need psychological help. Somatization reflects early upbringing, but indicates also a lack of a sense of security in relationships at home or at work. A man who has lost faith in his body has lost faith in his support system.

Chapter fourteen

Endpiece

Food is a man's life and clothes provide protection,
God gives him bounty, marriage provides cattle,
His wife is a friend, his daughter causes pity –
A son is like a light in highest heaven.

Anon. India 600 BC

Women want total freedom, or rather total licence.
If you allow them to achieve complete equality with
men, do you think they will be easier to live with?
Not at all. Once they have achieved equality they
will be your masters.

Cato 250 BC

I am woman, hear me roar
In numbers too big to ignore . . .
I am strong
I am invincible
I am woman.

Helen Reddy 1980

Men, in their concern to be top dogs, have subjugated women by
muscle power, denigration and denying them education, property or
position. But most of all the timeless tyranny of childbearing
hampered women – until the 1960s when Pincus developed the
completely effective, simple contraceptive pill. Before that only rare
women like Elizabeth I and Florence Nightingale retained control of
their lives, at the sacrifice of their sexuality. Now all women share

some of this freedom. Feminists are unfettered. Will males be pushed into subservience, become the weaker, lesser sex, with all the implications? Will it be the men who respond to second-class status by taking on domestic chores, cleaning the loo, and child care? Will it be men who weep and have neuroses? Already some firms grant paternity leave and there is a move afoot for fathers to take part-time work – to allow them more time in the home. Did Sir Norman Fowler give up high office for greater commitment to his young family because he is a new-style man? There is an increase in and acceptance of male homosexuality, in which men cook and housekeep for each other, exchange gifts of flowers, care obsessively about their appearance – and take overdoses. This may also be a portent of the new man.

Despite Cato's fears and improved female status, the main danger to psychological well-being and self-esteem for the human male does not come from women but from the inexorable advance of civilized living and domestication. As with the domestic dog, flabby muscles, sagging skin and hanging stomach, are now quite consistent with comfortable, 'successful' life. The releasing factors for eating and sex have hypertrophied while basic instincts about protecting the young and their mothers have atrophied. We are no longer greatly shocked by child abuse, rape and sexual murder. As in the domesticated animal coitus and reproduction are uncoupled, in their case by 'doctoring' to avoid unwanted puppies and kittens. Today's man selects his partner not for a capacious pelvis, adapted for childbirth, but a near-anorexic with narrow hips, who reliably takes the pill.

Another dangerous dissociation is between killing and the victim. Even shooting, which is low-tech, distances the aggressor from contact with blood, damage and death. This sidesteps the species-specific inhibition on killing common to other animals. Lions do not attack other lions: men have lost this safety factor. Despite the risks of technological advance leading the human species and the male in particular into physical and emotional calamity, there is a major saving grace in his inventiveness. All young animals, including our cousins the chimpanzees, are lively, inquisitive and playful. Lambs and piglets for example seem bright, intelligent and full of promise. Sadly these qualities fade with maturity in all creatures but man. As they grow up women cannot escape their cyclical hormonal activity, causing irrational premenstrual emotionality, abdominal discomfort and bleeding, reminders that they carry 99% of reproduc■ responsibility. Willy-nilly they settle into sensible adults. Men contrast, who have only to contribute coitus to posterity, are Nietzsche expresses: 'In the true man there is a child concealed, w wants to play.' The lively curiosity and playfulness of a man can ▮ all his life – to senility. This makes it possible, even probable, t▮ mankind will go on discovering and finding routes to survival. I▮ reassuring to see an adult male with his toys – talking to ▮ hand-phone in the street, roaring by on his motor-bike, playing bo▮ with his catamaran.

Of course both sexes are vital for continuance of the species a▮ individual contentment, but in very distinct ways.

The hope for the future, like the triumph of the past, lies in t▮ co-operation and complementarity of women and men.

Rosalind Miles 198▮